To John with very wishes love Anne

THE SELF REVEALED

Writing From Low Newton

Edited by
Wendy Robertson M.Ed

Published by Gemini Productions

ISBN 0-9532217-4-5

Book Design and Production: HPM Colour. 0191 300 6941

Front Cover 'Knot Wood' by Elaine Kenyon

Contents

Foreword

Early this year I was delighted to welcome author Wendy Robertson who joined us for an exceptional second term as HMP Low Newton's Writer In Residence.

I believe that much of the real work of a Writer In Residence goes unseen. I often meet Wendy, working with small groups of women or individuals, in our Learning Shop or in the small group room on F Wing, where she and her writers gather every Friday evening. However only now, as I am presented with The Self Revealed, this substantial collection of women's writing, do I understand the measure and nature of what she does. Now I realise how significant and inspirational her impact has been.

The range of work in this volume reflects the complex and individual nature of the women writers. In reading The Self Revealed we can all share and learn from this complexity and from the flowering of their creativity. In their writing the women reveal themselves in a way that does not find space in any other area of prison life. This makes it entirely unique.

The Self Revealed celebrates our women writers. It also celebrates the work of Wendy's residency. It is a mark of her enduring commitment to writing, and to the women of Low Newton, enabling them, as she does here, to find their true voice.

Paddy Fox
Governor
HMP Low Newton

Introduction

The Self Revealed showcases the work of Low Newton writers over recent months and includes poetry, short stories, memoirs and extracts from novels. The writing reveals honesty, authenticity and in some cases an amazing courage in trying to say the unsayable in a form that suggests emerging mastery, rather than victim-hood.

In this volume - as with all writers – we find that genuine wit, the language of imagination, and skills of invention can transform powerful life experiences from a curse into a resource, where truth can be handled at a safe critical distance. We have had many fruitful discussions about the crucial, liberating role fiction can play in this process.

As a matter of respect, I have included some of my own writing here, and that of Avril Joy, as we too are part of the community of writers at Low Newton, sharing a similar journey to become better writers.

In putting this collection together I have tried to avoid purely sentimental writing and focused on those writers who are continuing to grow and learn through their experience of writing. As a collection The Self Revealed communicates a broad range of insights, from which we in society can develop new kinds of understanding and empathy for the experience of individuals.

As well as this, it is a very good read: you may get angry, you may smile, you may cry, but you won't come away unmoved.

Wendy Robertson
Writer-in-Residence
Low Newton
www.wendyrobertson.com

Acknowledgements

I would like most of all to thank the talented writers of Low Newton who have invested such faith and trust in the writing process and offered their work and wisdom to be included in this important volume. We are all proud of the talent and insight they display here. I would especially thank Nicola and Ann Marie who, as well as contributing their writing talent to this book, have acted as an editorial sounding board in the development of this book.

Thank you to Avril Joy, Head of Learning and Skills at Low Newton, and Lesley Dixon, and her colleagues in the Learning Shop and the library, for providing me with the tolerant and creative framework in which to work. This has been so important in the complicated process of encouraging and facilitating original writing from talented people who are under stress. Thanks are also due the charity New Bridge, who support the Learning Shop, for their invaluable support in the production of this book*.

Thank you to Governor Paddy Fox for welcoming me to Low Newton, and, busy as he is, finding time to express his appreciation of the work we writers have accomplished. Also thank you to author David Almond for his encouraging reading of this work.

Thank you to Gillian Wales for helping me with the editing and publishing process, and as always encouraging me to aspire for the best. And thank you to John Alderson at HPM for his support and technical expertise in the production of this book. A special thanks to Elaine Kenyon for allowing us to use her beautiful art work for the cover. Its pared back elegance acts as some kind of visual metaphor for women's lives. The Self Revealed, indeed.

A special and separate thanks to Avril Joy, whose writer's interest and pride in the women's work has made it possible to go one mile further.

Wendy Robertson
Durham
2007

*See New Bridge & The Learning Shop p142

The Corridor

AC

My first time in prison,
I'm placed on 'I' Wing,
A totally new environment for me,
A pad of my own,
Unfamiliar faces staring at me,
They have already formed a special bond,
How will the inmates be with me?
I ready myself for First Movement,
As I walk, dragging my feet apprehensively,
Over to the bigger barred building,
I don't know what to expect,
The noises bombard my ears,
The jingling of keys, slamming of doors,
Shouts, screams, laughter, aggression,
Bravado, the walk of power in sight,
Anxiety washes over me,
Don't know where to focus or put myself,
I queue quietly and courteously,
Afraid to speak up,
To the well known queue jumpers,
As time passes by, my fear drifts.
That big barred building isn't scary after all,
The whitewash of paint gives a clinical look,
Not everyone now is as mad as I thought,
I can see me doing my time with ease,
My friends, my special bond of friends,
Will help me through this difficult time.

First Day

NR

I got to the jail and in I went
So this is where everybody's sent
Into reception I was told to go
Now what's going to happen
I really don't know
Into a room with some other girls
Some with straight hair
Some with curls
I get called out and asked to strip
Do I have to do this after that long trip?
Then stand in. Front here!
Stand still and Look!
A flash blinds my eyes
And I have my photo took.
Into another room I go
I've had enough I want to go
'Would you like something to eat? Some tea?
I say, 'I'm not hungry thank you, no.'

In came two officers with kind faces
To put us through what must be the paces
We follow them out through a small gate
I wonder now, what will be my fate.
Down to the wing we all go
I soon learn the ropes and get stuck in
Why oh why did I commit that sin?
I'm in here now and must do my time
I'll never again commit that crime

Visitation

AP

It's strange how you come to believe in things that you didn't before or never thought that you would. Just by something strange happening or the unknown to happen. In my case it was that I had a guardian angel or ghost of some kind looking out for me.

I was eight months pregnant with my fourth child and was in hospital due to having quite a lot of pain and generally having a bad time of it with this child. It was one of the worst pregnancies I'd ever had. I was having trouble sleeping and was having quite a few restless nights, but this one night I will never forget as long as I live.

I woke up with a start and tried to sit up but I couldn't as I had a sharp pain in my side. So I lay gently back down and was lying on my side. I was thinking that maybe I should try to reach the call button and ring for a nurse, but I just closed my eyes and tried to think about things good in my life, other than this aching pain that was going on. But hard as I tried it wasn't going away any time soon and I just started to cry. I had these crazy thoughts running through my head that something was wrong with the baby and that I should be ringing for some help not just laying here crying.

I tried to pull myself together and reach up for the control so that I could call for a nurse to come, but something strange caught my eye at the end of the bed. I really thought I was dreaming and maybe that I was still asleep. I kept shutting and opening my eyes and yet I couldn't take my eyes of what I was seeing.

So what was I seeing? I was sure it was a woman, just a faded glow of an older woman at the end of the bed. She had a soft glow around her, yet my room was pitch black. I looked around her, trying to see if my room door was open and if I could see the light and that this was just a nurse coming to do her rounds. I blinked again and just stared still with the tears still running down my face, and crazy as it sounds I wasn't scared or anything just confused at what I was seeing.

Then she spoke to me. You could hardly hear what she was saying and I could only just make it out.

'Turn over.'

'Turn over.'

This was said a few times yet I just lay there staring.

Then I heard my name. Not what I get called now but a name that I had when I was little. Not a lot of people knew this name.

'Esna, Turn over'

I was scared now as there had only really been one person who said Esna the way I was hearing it. This was my grandmamma and she was dead. She died when I was little. I started to cry again and was sobbing so hard it hurt, yet I did as I was told and turned over, even though the pain that ripped through me was unbearable. I could still see this lady who I believed to this day was my late grandmamma.

Just as I was getting up the nerve to speak to her she started to fade and I could hear her words. 'He's safe now. He's safe now.' Then she - or whatever I had seen - was gone. Just like that. As if I had just imagined it all, but I knew I hadn't either that or I had just gone bonkers.

Then I grabbed the control and I pushed the call button for the nurse. I must have looked weird as I told her what had just happened and about the awful pain I had been having in my stomach and that I had managed to turn over.

She went out and came back with a doctor and the mobile scan monitor. That's when it all went crazy and the doctor started barking orders out. A few moments later I was being rushed into theatre and was about to be put under for an emergency caesarean section, but I wanted to know what was going on and shouted that they were all frightening me. I begged them to tell me and was shocked at the news. My baby had the cord wrapped around its neck and that if they didn't get it delivered the baby would die. But the next bit of news scared me even more as he just told me that if I hadn't turned over when I did then my baby would have died and the fact I turned over meant the cord loosened a bit around its neck.

Now I have not said the sex of the baby as yet as this was the other amazing thing that had happened as I hadn't asked what my baby's sex was or even been told. And yes, my baby was a boy just like she said and yes, he was safe. So who was this lady that I saw and do I believe that she was my late grandmamma? Yes I honestly think it was and that she was my guardian angel, who looks over my life and that of my children.

My grandmamma's name is also Esna. She was Egyptian and

there is a great belief there, that of being named after your grandparents and a gift of spiritual belonging comes with it.

My grandmamma knew I was needing her, and she was there in spirit that's for sure.

Barbridge

C

The splashing of fish
The cows mooing in the distant field
The tractor at the far end
Hello Duck! Shshshsh!
(Whispering) Any luck?
M6 Flyover – North-South
Where do you fancy going today?
Fishing
Go and see Farmer Giles at the Swamp
People say it's a good place to fish
I say it's beautiful

Friday 11am

NR

Fast as a bullet
Speedier than light
Adrenalin pumping
Blood rushing
Excitement building
Gas draining
Road shaking
Horns honking
Corner turning
Starting to slide
Slipping and swaying
Closing in
Crash bang wallop
Car ploughs
Into a house

The Joker

JJ

As she sits shuffling the cards
The dealer's face is cold and hard
Knowing she is in command
Slowly she deals my hand
The King The Jack The Queen The Ace
Are life's pleasures that we face
The happiness, the cheerful times
The love that makes relationships bind
But the ten, the nine, the eight
Represent all the things we hate
The arguments the constant fights
Isolation on cold, wintry nights
And what of the seven, the six, the five?
They question why we're stick alive
They are the problems of bills and debts
Addictions of alcohol, the need to bet
Next come the four, the three, the two
The people we lose, the things we must do
The death of a loved one, the grieving, the loss
The pros and the cons, the counting of costs.
The joker's the only one saving the game
In two deals of life it's never the same
It can be what it wants, changing the hand
Destroying the game the dealer had planned
I've got two tens, an ace and a six
Proving that debt and relationships don't mix
With the death of my mum and my son too
I've surely a four as well as a two.
Whoever's the dealer, life's cards are a sod
Making me question the dealer is God
I'd want a new hand if this were poker
But in this game I'm the Joker

Early Morning Blue

How come I'm such a sinner then...

Novel Extract 1

AMJ

Chapter 1

Not a wisp or a curl, not a trail or a smudge, not a trace of cloud, only blue, but you can never see the whole of it, not from this window.

They call me Theresa. Theresa Doyle, that's my name, T for short, sometimes, especially in here. My mother chose it. It was after her favourite saint, the 'Little Flower,' Marie Françoise Therese Martin. She worshipped her and kept her picture next to the bed in a pink plastic frame decorated with roses. My mother lived in hope that I would grow up sweet and pure just like Saint Theresa. Well I hate to disappoint but pure I most definitely am not, and I'm no sweet pea either.

Bless her, but what the fuck did she know?

When my mother gave up, when she finally abandoned her hope, like a beaten up old box left out in the rain, she abandoned me or to put it another way, she passed on, as they say. She died. By then I was fifteen and old enough to look after myself so that was okay and besides I'd met Landy and we had set out on our summer of love. But that's not to say I don't miss her still, every day. Or that I've ever stopped loving her. Or wishing it had been different.

How come I'm such a sinner then, what with my holy name and all? What makes someone like me the rotten apple, the black sheep, the sinner not the saint? I can't answer that. You'll have to make up your own mind. I don't go in too much for all that psychobabble. The way I see it, it's my responsibility to look after myself and keep things right and if they're not, well I'm the one to blame, no one else.

Saint Theresa promised the world a shower of roses when she died. She died young, she was only twenty-four. I'm twenty-three and I'm promising nothing. Not that I'm planning on dying, not yet, anyway, but I should warn you - in this place, death is only ever a breakfast away.

Longmoor sits on the flat lands beside a river, somewhere east,

I don't know where. Hot on the inside, hot as hell, and cool on the out, like an ice cream pie, the kind you bake, only the other way round, inside out, if you know what I mean. Outside damp, morning mists wind round us like the confessional lace. Inside the temperature's turned up to the max, to keep us switched off and slow. To keep us sweet, as we wilt under the screaming light. Don't even try to guess why we're here, why I'm here, well not yet anyway, we all have our secrets, we need them, and besides you'll get to know soon enough. Wait. It is all about waiting.

Now, before lunch bang-up, is my time. When the door closes the cell presses her body against mine. Her eye, bulges and flickers like a fat toad's, watching me. She sees everything. She pounds in my head and presses on my chest but I know it won't be long. I breathe hard and wait. I wait for what I know will come, for the space to grow, for the walls to slip away. I wait for a cathedral of space to grow around me until I'm small, floating like a speck of dust caught in the pale light. I breathe out, slow and long. Fuck, that's better.

I fill my sink with water and add a capful of sticky, pink, fabric softener. It smells of old roses. I soak the j cloth, squeeze it out and begin my cleaning. I do this at lunchtime, every day; there isn't time in the morning. I start with the walls, where I can. I wipe in slow circles, soft circles of comfort. I find the dust in hidden corners where it lays on the thick collars of pipes and I wipe it away.

I shake the bedclothes, smooth the duvet and the pillow ready to lie down. I sprinkle them with talc to take away the smell. I don't like thinking about the others who've slept here – their body fluids, their dead skin, hairs like the ones you see blocking the showers, stains like spilt tea on the pillow, stains dribbled from medicated mouths, self or otherwise. I want to wash them all away.

That's where the canteen comes in. The canteen is a lifeline, toiletries, stuff for washing, you ask anyone, anyone with any self respect, anyone but a junkie (and even some junkies):coconut conditioner, lilac shampoo, strawberry face wash, coca butter body cream, deodorant sticks, roll ons, (no sprays), blue hair gel, almond moisturiser; good enough to eat, better than the crap they dish up in here.

And while we're on the subject of lifelines there's the library too, that's another lifeline, well for me anyway. I read most things, anything, though not True Crime like a lot in here. I really need my books. Just now I'm reading Bob Dylan Chronicles Volume 1 - it's on the shelf next to my apricot shower gel - odd, I hear you say, for someone my age, weird, but I recognise his words, because my mother, Bernadette, that was her name, she liked his songs and she played them a lot.

On my desk, under the window, are two oranges on a white plastic plate. I keep them like a prize, like satsumas from a Christmas stocking. I like to roll them about in my hands and rub the skin with my thumb. One of them is drying out and starting to wrinkle up but the other one is still scented and fresh. If I hold it up to my nose I can smell the marmalade she put on her toast.

Do you know an orange is not orange? No, an orange will most likely have patches of pink and yellow and even green, if you look close enough, if you screw up your eyes like I sometimes do. You see, things are not always what we say or what they seem. They're just not that simple. I've learned that. In the corridors, outside the cells, there are skins thicker than ten jaffa oranges and masks made of concrete... fuck it....oranges are all very well but I'd rather be out there looking at the sky. Wouldn't you? I roll the orange, the one that's still fresh, against my cheek and under my nose then open my book... 'You gotta learn how to bluff. You'll never make it in this game if you don't...'

Mandy's stood in front of me in the dinner queue, Mandy Crumb. She needs new clothes. Her belly rolls like a sausage over the top of her jeans back and front. The waistband digs in. Her skin is red and sore looking. She smiles when she sees me and puts her arm around my shoulder and her head into my chest. I put my arms around her. I wish I could do something about her clothes, I wish I could do something about the giant hole inside her that she fills with food, anything she can get her hands on.I wish I could magic away the white gauze dressings on her arms. Mandy's arms are purple and red and blue and the skin hangs like crepe paper, lined and loose with a lifetime of cutting. Dressings are good, though – a good sign, cause at least someone has cleaned her cuts, stitched them maybe, rubbed cream along the puckered ridges of old scars. Someone has been gentle. Times I've seen Mandy's arms and had to look away. I couldn't do that to myself, but plenty women in here do, and just to stay alive.

She's restless, hopping from one foot to another, medication, anticipation? It's hard to know which because Mandy's usually medicated to the max, provided she hasn't sold her meds that is, or swapped them or given them away for a packet of chocolate biscuits. She is in the meds queue morning, noon and night, along with half the jail. And then in the breakfast queue, she's usually one of the first, filling that giant hole, keeping her hunger monster at bay. The screws know she keeps food in her pad. She hoards it. Mostly they turn a blind eye as long as it doesn't get out of hand, because there's the hygiene to think of, the rats and cockroaches which none of us want, although I doubt Mandy cares. I often give her titbits, save her the chocolate biscuits especially.

' Theresa,' her voice muffles into my chest. She sounds like a kid of no more than ten, she smells of piss, she looks up at me, 'You all right?'

'I'm fine, you?'

'Going to chapel this afternoon, bible group with Monica'

'That's good,' I say and mean it.

'Yeh, it's jaffa cakes on Thursdays.'

'That'll be nice, your favourite aren't they?'

' Yeah, I suppose jaffa cakes are my favourite. I like custard creams though.'

I wonder, if I pray to Saint Theresa, will she shower the world in jaffa cakes and custard creams? I'd love to see Mandy's face.

I put my arm around her and say, 'Yeah I like custard creams too.' I push her gently towards the servery and the smell of meat pie, then say,' Fuck, gotta go back, I've forgotten that address for Angela.' And I leave her and go back into the corridor heading for the toilets where I duck in and wash my hands. Twice.

I was doing six months the winter I met Mandy, it was only my second time. This is my third and the longest by far, but it's nearly over now. Only thirty seven breakfasts to go.

It's the middle of March, spring, not that you'd know it, except when you're at work, if you work outside that is, like I do. Most of the time in here one season's the same as another and best forgotten a lot would say. But I don't forget. I look for the changes in the odd shaped pieces of sky between the roofs and the razor wire. I smell them on the thin air. Even in here there's no disguising the seasons; the slip into autumn when wood smoke and wet grass lurk under the scent of bodies and polish, and you can tell when spring's coming too, like now, with the wallflowers in the greenhouse and the birds in the morning. But in here what difference does it really make? Fucking, fuck all, I suppose, when you think about it.

Out there, it makes plenty of difference.

Out there when it was summer Landy and me slept under the stars and life was easy. I heard my mother talk about it – the summer of love, it was sometime in the sixties when everyone wore flowers in their hair and badges that said make love not war and walked about smoking spliffs. It stuck with me, came back to me the summer after I met Landy. That was my summer of love.

We met at School. He had the kind of face that cried out for love, you know the sort; soft, a baby face with sad green eyes and a body like a greyhound, fragile and thin. He needed looking after and so did I. She was already ill and any fool could see it was serious and she wasn't going to get better. We spent the whole of that summer in each other's arms, out on the water meadows, in the lush grasses, with the buttercups and the weepy-eyed cows.

Then when the green grew tired and leaves started to lie about, all sodden on the grass we left the meadows and ran away for good. By then she was gone and there was nothing to stay put for so we ran to the town by the sea.

We scavenged wood and old bits of furniture from back alleys to take back to our squat. We built a fire that never went out from November through to February, Landy made sure of that, ashing it over every night. Out there your survival is all winter and cold, it lasts no more than six months. In here it's all the time and there's nowhere much to run, but there are ways....

The first time I stepped into a cell, and heard the weight of the handle locking the door, I couldn't breathe. My lungs seized, my throat choked and I had to press the bell. They came running then and opened the door and brought me a brown paper canteen bag to breathe into. They sat with me for a while, sat next to me on the rock of a mattress and waited 'til I was breathing again okay. Then they left, and locked me back in and that's when I had to learn and learn fast, how to unhook from the past, how to live in the now or better still, somewhere else, because one thing you can be sure of; your past will haunt you in a cell. If you don't believe me then you try it. See what monsters lurk in the corners and beneath the bed waiting for you. That first time, once I could breathe, after they left I crouched on the floor and put my arms over my head and I heard his laughing and felt the cracking fist in my face, the one that snapped the young bones in my nose, the one that showed me what a good hiding was.

I learned fast about being locked up, how imagination is your curse and your saviour and I learned not to fuck about with it. It's like with any weapon, you need to know what you're doing, you need to take control, make it your friend. So you might see me here, if you put your eye to the spy hole, like a screw would, or if you lifted the viewing flap and used both eyes. I might be lying reading on my bed, and you might think you see me, but believe me, you don't. Remember, things are not always what they seem. First time round a woman, a lifer, said to me, 'They can take away your freedom but they can never take away your mind. 'It stuck with me. It's true.It's what distinguishes me, from you, my gaoler. It's what keeps me human and alive.

From my window…"S" Wire, scaffolding poles, a roof under repair, voices, men's, I think, I can't make out the words, the slamming of metal against metal, the brutal crack of iron gates. Someone is laughing, key chains rattle as they are drawn from pockets and green guttering glows at the lit windows of cells. It's growing dark, early like it does still at the winter's end, spring dark, slow dark. I look at the blue above me, on my ceiling, the torn patch from the colour supplement of some newspaper, stuck on and blue as blue, like the sky seen from a picnic in the dunes.

The sea laps and slaps at the bed's feet. I close my eyes and smell the salt on the marshes and feel the rough grass scratch at my legs and catch in my ankle socks. We only went there on sunny days: that must be why the sky lives blue and cloudless in my head

'Bernadette…..Bernadette.'

'What?' She is busy taking off her socks and shoes and making herself comfortable.

'Where's my paper?'

'I don't know.'

'Well you packed the frigging bag didn't you? You must know woman.'

'I don't. Theresa, here, you can't play in those, get them off and put this costume on.' My skin prickles at the thought of a wet bathing costume caked with sand.

'Suppose I'd better bloody look myself then you useless cow.'

'Suppose you'd better.' She winked at me and I held my breath.

'What about a sandwich then?' he said after a pause. She smiled at me.

They were happy times. Out in the open.

(If you like this, try the second chapter p105)

Mum!

NR

I miss your laughter
I miss your smile
I miss not seeing you
For such a long while
I miss the way you make me feel
I know I owe you a great deal

You've always been there
When I was lonely and scared
Thank you for the things you've done for me
You're the whole world, the moon and the sun

What would I have done
If you weren't there?
All you've ever done is care
One day I'll be with you
And we will have fun
Cause I couldn't ask
For a better mum

Hearts

AMG

When I look up I see
The strangely twisted, razor wire hearts
Linked in empathy.
They are so beautiful
As they catch the autumn sun in their barbs
Holding on to it
Like a desperate lover.
Is my own heart up there?
I lost it along time ago.
Maybe, it is that one on the end
Reaching out into nothingness.

The Mythical Mother

Short Story

JJ

The following was found propped up against a television.

To whom it may concern.

I am writing so that you may have some understanding – an explanation if you like. Hopefully it will explain to you why I'm doing what I'm doing. Ultimately it may answer the question why.

I've been in this hell now for over seven years but that's only part of it. The walls around me are nothing now. Nothing compared to the cold emptiness I feel inside.

I can remember when life was good. Perfect, even.

I remember my children: playing, laughing, and sleeping peacefully. I remember all three of them. My perfect, magical little ones. I remember my husband. The love we shared. The strength he gave me. The plans we had then are not even a memory. They are a dream. Surely I was never that happy. My life could not have been that perfect such a short time ago. I know in my heart that it was but my brain doesn't seem to believe it. It's too painful to let myself believe.

I know me and Phil had our difficulties but I really thought we'd got past that. And then, when Sarah was born, everything seemed ideal. My life finally on the right track. My Phil and I there together and now we'd had our third baby. We were even planning to buy our house. We started our home improvement plans: laid a lawn, decorated the house inside and out, enrolled George at school and got our Theresa into a nursery. That summer we'd booked a holiday – two weeks in Cornwall. It was nothing grand but it was our first holiday as a complete family.

Why is it that life rarely goes the way you've planned? Why did things go the way they did? Why don't I have any answers?

When Sarah died that summer my world fell apart. How could I possibly carry on? How could I only mother two when I should have three? How could I not be angry? I had so many questions then and no one seemed to have any answers for me.

I was lucky. I had Phil. He tried to comfort me, to understand in the pain I was feeling. But in the end he couldn't cope with me any more. I wasn't the woman he had married. He kept telling me that. He couldn't understand that I couldn't be that person any more. Sarah's death had changed me. I was scared. Terrified. I was angry. But mostly I was confused. In the end Phil took the children and moved out. He tried to stop me seeing them. I didn't know what was worse, having a child die, or having two children alive and not being allowed to see them. I couldn't imagine life getting worse then. I truly believed my life was at its lowest point.

No such luck, though.

Three months after Sarah died, two months after Phil walked out, the police walked in. I was charged with Sarah's death. I was dragged from hell and thrown into something much worse. They really believed I killed her. How could they? Couldn't they see how perfect she was? How she made my life, my family complete?

I won't bother detailing the failures of my legal team. Or the injustice of my trial and its outcome. That has all been covered before in the media and in my journal.

That year on bail was hard: not knowing whether I'd see George and Theresa again; feeling strange everywhere I went. The world wasn't real any more. How could it be when the most important parts of it had been taken from me? I wandered around the house imagining, remembering, their laughter, their warmth. I would spend hours in one place – the bathroom, the garden, the stairs – trying desperately to recapture memories of when they were there.

I remembered how effective, when I decorated George and Theresa's bedroom. They were only four and two years old and they wanted to help. Theresa wanted to help with the painting so I gave her an empty paint-pot and a clean brush and asked her to paint the skirting board. She loved it and felt proud that she'd decorated her own bedroom.

George had the job of sanding. She armed herself with Phil's sanding block and set to work on one of the cupboards. That memory still brings tears. Just like the day they asked if they could polish the wooden floor of the dining room. I explained to them how much work was involved and I suggested they should polish the wooded furniture instead. I really thought they would only do one piece but how wrong I was. George polished the furniture while Theresa swept the floor. Then, bless them, they started to polish the floor on their hands and knees. They wouldn't even accept my help. They put me on 'tea duty' – clearly a phrase picked up from their dad.

Every room of that house has their mark on it. Some wonderful memory that haunts me still. But they are just memories, precious, hurtful memories. I try so hard not to remember Sarah because of the pain. But lately though she is all I can think about. Every minute of every day my thoughts are with her: splashing in her bath, her little hands slapping the water as she giggles. Her sun-drenched face, smiling as she lies on the lawn wearing nothing but a nappy and a smile. Her smile could light the darkest place.

How could they think I had killed her?

They think that sticking me in prison will be hard for me. That I will repent. How can I? How can I show remorse when I have committed no crime? They do not understand and they fail to hear my maintenance of innocence.

In truth though, it doesn't matter. It doesn't matter that they lock me in this cold hard cell 23 hours a day. It does not matter that I am subjected to abuse or discrimination. They cannot hurt me. Nothing can hurt me more than I already hurt. It doesn't matter what they do to me. I know physical pain is temporary. It's the emotional pain that lasts forever – the pain of having all your children taken from you; the pain of knowing two of them are barred from seeing you most of the time.

Not absolutely though. I sometimes wonder if not seeing them at all would be easier for all of us. If they were told I was dead they wouldn't keep asking the questions I can't answer. Why don't you live with us? When will you come home?

They deserve answers even if the answer is I'm never coming home because I'm dead.

As it is they are left thinking I don't love them. I never go to their school plays. I wasn't at their parents' evening. I don't celebrate their birthdays with them. I never do anything with them. All they are allowed from me is the occasional phone call. Thirteen a year. And even fewer letters. I am a mythical mother, a shadow over their young lives, always lurking in their minds but never physically there in their lives. Just like Sarah, little more than a photograph.

Sarah. My beauty. All alone. Still not buried, her body still in the coroner's mortuary. Waiting. Waiting for more tests to find out why she died. Not for my sake. Getting out of prison is never going to happen for me because even when I leave this physical prison I still have the torturous realm of my mind. The only reason I search for an explanation is for her. She deserves the world to know that she was truly loved. That she was so perfect and precious. How else can her spirit rest?

And so it is after almost nine years that she still hasn't had her day of passing. I know though that if I give up my fight she will have that day. Nobody else would continue the fight. Nobody cares like I do. Nobody else knows how much she was loved. How much she still is loved.

So you see, all of my babies are sturdy in turmoil. All of them have pain: George my sturdy little fighter, sturdy and practical; Theresa, my beautiful little girl, the protector. And Sarah my princess. They have a burden to carry, and that burden is me.

I hope beyond hope that my death will release them from that pain. It will free them to continue their journeys, finally give them some answers to their questions. Sarah will be able to have her final day. I know that everyone says that death is the easy way out. Trust me, it's not. I will die knowing I did not find the reason for Sarah's death. I will die knowing the world believes I killed her because I didn't love her. Death is hard to embrace with a smile. So no, I haven't made this choice lightly. And yes I have thought about it for a long time.

All I ask of you is that you contact my solicitor. She has a letter detailing the arrangements for Sarah's day.

I have one more thing to ask of you. In years to come if George and Theresa ask why, tell them. Tell them I did it because they deserve better than me. Tell them they deserve better than the life I could give them. Tell them I love them.

As I sit here taking these pills, each one represents a loving memory: a memory with George, Theresa and Sarah. They are in my thoughts, my heart and my soul.

Yours truly,
Marianne

The Death of Me

AMG

Long, lean, almond coloured limbs,
Dressed in a pretty striped dress;
Looking so innocent.
A smile that reveals perfectly spaced, even teeth.
A vicious bite!
Suddenly becoming alive.
We tussle, we struggle we tangle up;
I have lost again.
She is always the winner.
One day, this deckchair will be the death of me!

Hot Coffee

NR

I take a hold of you
I try and sip you slowly
I blow hard into you
I try another sip from you
I get burned so I blow once more
I'm determined to drink you hot
I take a hold of you again
I can feel your heat through the cup
I take another sip
But god damn I've burnt my lip
I put you down and try to wait
But the urge to pick you up again takes over
I blow and blow until finally I stop
And take another sip
But god damn you I've burnt my lip again
I hold the cup and just blow and blow some more
I'm so thirsty I want to drink you so much
Finally I use my head and add cold water
Finally I drink you gulp after gulp you go down
And then comes disappointment because now you're all gone

Intruders

Short Story

XH

She hears a noise like somebody was walking around the lounge, Her weary mind suddenly stirs her body is atremble. It is raining and windy outside. The curtains are constantly moved by the hand of the wind. The gleam of a headlight pierces in and out as the curtains wave. She can't tell how many people there are because the wind is howling in the trees outside.

She's pretty sure her bedroom is locked from the inside, so she stretches her hand out to search for the button of the lamp. As soon as the light is on the noise stops. No matter whether they are human beings or ghosts they have noticed she is here now.

Her mind just stops working. Reacting to the stopped noise she switches the lamp back off, What a fool she is. This has only brought their attention to her again because she can hear them again, hanging around. She lies still for nearly five minutes which seems a very long time. Her gown becomes impregnated with sweat.

What can she do? She has to find the phone to call the police before they do something bad to her. They are still busy in the lounge even now. Now the stupid woman switches on the lamp again. Now the uncanny intruders stop again. It is driving her insane.

As she crept to her coat to find the phone she could hear them scratching through a chink in the door. Finally overcome by curiosity she opened the door. There, scrambling on the floor was a crab: one of the five she bought last night for dinner that were now creeping everywhere over the lounge.

Trust

NR

What is trust in a place like this?
This that and the other, no bliss
Say one thing and it gets repeated
It gets turned inside out
And then mistreated
You can't trust no-one –
Not even yourself
Even if all of it's true
A so-called friend, they don't give a fuck
So I'll stay in my pad, write, read a book
From now on I'll do my own thing
Cause I can't cope with that backstabbing wing

Feeling lonely all on my own
Can't even talk on the phone
They push and they shove
They all kick and scream
Please tell me now it's all a bad dream
But this dream isn't going away
I try not to worry cause I'll be out one day
When I'm out of them gates
No looking back, I'm off on my skates
Won't ever come back no more.

Dark Angel

Short Story

AMG

Sally South bought herself a flower for her much beloved garden, the first pure black sweet pea – Dark Angel. It was launched at the Chelsea flower show

It had exquisite blooms, large waxy bat ears, impossibly supported on slender, sage coloured stems. But the most sensational aspect of this new discovery was the scent, addictive, heady and intoxicating. One flower could perfume a whole room. This wonder plant was also hardy. It could thrive in any conditions and withstand both drought and frost. Wherever the seeds were planted, they germinated and flourished. It truly was the talk of the horticultural world, the plant of the century for sure.

What was even more remarkable was that no one had taken credit for it, the first seeds had been sent anonymously to an international seed company and the rest was history.

Sally had felt unwell with flu-like symptoms and nose bleeds for several days before she visited her doctor in Kensington. He prescribed antibiotics and told her to come back in a few days if the bleeds continued. She never returned. A week later she was dead.

There were more cases all over the country, then in other parts of the world. Autopsies could not identify the mystery virus. Work continued frantically to find a drug to control this dreadful epidemic as more and more died.

The fanatical scientist smiled to himself, he was all powerful now. He was God! Ha, that was a good one, a scientist playing God, but this was no game, he held all the cards. Only he knew what was causing the mass destruction of the human race, he alone had the answer which he would never reveal.

He sat back in his chair admiring the great love of his life, his magnificent garden, and breathed in deeply the smell of the Dark Angel.

Getting Ready

XH

The water is rolling down her fringe. A flush is reflecting on her cheeks. She pushes the door open and comes into the room. The presenter is still busy on the breakfast news. As she watches she is putting on body cream and face cream. She enjoys turning round and letting the air dry her body.

She opens the wardrobe where all her clothes are ironed and folded. She picks up one purple top and puts it back. Her hand is touching a grey one but then she chooses a bright pink tee-shirt and her favourite jeans. She loves being well dressed, no matter what the occasion. Being well-dressed and wearing make-up gives her confidence and tranquility.

She goes downstairs to make some toast and takes it back to her room. Every morning she sits in the window drinking strong coffee and making toast while she watches the cars come and go in the road. The sun strokes her face and the wind flirts with her hair.

Today she is going to chapel instead of Education. At nine o'clock a woman comes to take her and another two women to chapel. They pray and sing for an hour then they start reading the Bible, the holy book of the world.

My God I couldn't tell where she was.

She is in prison.

The Red Snapper

Group

Swimming in the salty sea
Shooting sparks electric blue
Glittering with shining scales
Silver set on green and black
Bubble-streaming open mouth
Swimming-slipping through the coral
Icthus[1] moving through life's water

But now he dangles on a hook
Wriggling, giving off a salty smell
Now, his eyes are sad and empty
Knowing he will soon be scaled,
Dressed with lemons
Served up in crispy batter

And knowing that he won't decay
Before he's eaten

[1] *Icthus is the Greek word for fish. The fish symbol was adopted by early Christians as a secret sign, due to persecution. (This word was Sarah's inspiration)*

The Sea

JJ

I know you feel you have been cast adrift in a tempestuous sea, left to float on the current, alone and unaided, battered by the tide's fancy. As it thrashes against the rocky cliffs you stay battened to your raft of strength and the violent sea persists in trying to abnegate you, dragging you fighting and screaming below its dark embrace.

The anger and violence bombard you, drenching your clothes, seeping through to your skin. You rise and fall to the random flow of the storm, The encapsulated current, the dark vastness astounds you with no hope of sanctuary, no visible escape.

Only the sharks, slicing through the water around you, are a means of respite. They will consume you whole. The sharp teeth will pierce your body, tear your flesh: daggers of pain deaden parts of you. Killing you.

But still, their hunger is welcoming, You crave release from the torrential sea: violence meets violence; cold isolation destroyed by the coldness of death: the freedom to sacrifice your longing for help with the finality of a shark; an escape from your confining battens.

Far off, a mermaid, a siren of the sea, ready to give you your escape, your freedom. If only she could draw near but the shark blocks her again. She swims gracefully in calming waters on the periphery of your vision, her gentle strokes soothing the sea. She longs to reach you, to guide you back to land, to free you from your confines.

But you feel safe, secure in the predictable knowledge of sharks, accepting the violent release from stormy waters. And as she swims into the edge of view the mermaid watches your raft as it is engulfed by the tide clutched by the sea as you are dragged into the water's rage, the surface closing over you.

Love is …

R

Love is one of the strongest things in the world
Love has destroyed lives
Love has made hate
Love is the feeling people use to commit murder
Love makes revenge
Love causes divorce
Love separates families
People die for love
People live for love
Love makes you stronger
Love makes you cry
Love makes you smile
Love makes you sigh, makes your chest swell
Love gives you energy
Love makes you love

Anger In My Eyes

TP

I look at her with anger in my eyes, after what she has just said. I can't believe it. You know its like when you have had a bad dream and you feel that screaming fear in your throat but you can't make a noise no matter how hard you try. That's what it was like. Then there's that incredible relief when you wake up and it's all gone, you're safe again, or safe as you can be while in here, but this time I didn't feel safe. I just wanted to get away, anywhere just as far away from her as I could.

It wasn't her fault, not really, she didn't know. How, how could she? Or she wouldn't have said it out loud like she did, about her abuse, what she had gone through. I can't understand people like her, how they can speak so openly and to me come over so flippant. It's stupid, they're stupid, don't they know that's not normal, how can they do that? How can I believe them, her!

No if it had happened to her, then she would have kept it quiet, too scared to talk, not be so blasé about it all. She would have hidden it, be ashamed about it and hate herself. No it's definitely not normal, she is not normal. She can't be.

You see me, I hate myself. So much I'm in fear even now just hearing her words coming from her mouth, and I'm back in that nightmare. I'm there crying and trying so hard not to make a noise, just silent sobs. He's coming for me, I can hear his footsteps, his heavy breathing, him calling my name in a singsong sort of voice. My terror is so real. I can't breathe. My throat tightens. Its hurting now with having to keep my crying muffled. Then I hear screaming and it won't stop, my eyes open and I'm awake, with tears streaming down my face, my skin clammy. I sit up and hug my knees to my body, I look around, and I'm in my cell. I know I won't be going back to sleep, not tonight.

Yes I was safe, hard to believe that I'm in prison and yet it is the safest place I've been for a long time in my life, for now.

Loneliness

NR

Locked up in a blanket of loneliness
That makes my insides shake
Feelings of abandonment, of years gone by return
Sitting alone waiting for company that never comes
Wanting to be held or just feel loved for a little while
So sick of this never-ending loneliness
Watching TV that's the only company for me

Lying down wrapped in my blanket of loneliness
So alone it hurts deep inside
Desperate and full of hurt so I cut up inside
To cover up the loneliness inside my head
Why oh why can no one see my cry

So not just stay
and lay
in my blanket
of loneliness

Obsession

AMG

They have a voice all of their own and they call out to me,
'Take me home mummy don't leave me in this cold window'.
How can I resist? I already have a large family, but another addition will fit in nicely.
I have no prejudice, all colours are welcome: black, brown, yellow, and white. I am a broody hen, always on the lookout for my next chic little ones.
There are, of course, my favourites, but I treat all my dear ones with the same loving care and attention.
No neglect in my household!
I am always proud to be seen out in public with them.
Yes, I do have an obsession.
The lady loves her shoes

My House

AMJ

Crying of newly born lambs
Out in the winter night
Hum of the boiler beneath the stairs
Hi, hello honey babe
Witton Bank Cemetery Row
There's fresh tea in the pot
People say this is a good place to bring up children
I think … maybe …it was.

Summertime Blues

AP

It was summertime early June and it was quite a hot day, so we decided to have a barbeque outside in the garden. Elie my partner was staying over at the time and this was our first barbeque together as a couple with my kids and his son.

We had set the pool up and we were all just starting to settle down after a lovely day. I'd just put my youngest kids to bed and was in the kitchen having another glass of wine, whilst tidying up everything, when the phone rang.

'Toni, phone for you' Elie shouts, 'it's your kid Sam' I remember having a chuckle to myself at how Elie spoke, it's always your or our kid when talking about family.

It's crazy at how you remember the small details, even the smells, in my case the barbeque, the sweet smell of the wine and my Elie's aftershave Joop. And at how that one phone call changed my life so dramatically.

'Sam where you been hiding? I've been trying to reach you for days, what's up?' Why didn't I notice then, at how strange he sounded, like he didn't even sound like my brother, it was more like a hollow and automatic like a robot talking to me.

Then he dropped the bombshell 'Esna, Mum's dead,'

The crazy thing is I haven't been called Esna by Sam since I was a kid and we didn't call mum, mum, it was usually Esna (my mum's name, which was why I changed my name). It was very rarely we even talked about her, so I should have realised it was true even then, just with those three little words. But I really didn't believe him at al.

Then I remembered hearing him repeat it. 'Mum's dead'.

I don't know what it was at first, but I could hear this strange noise, it was getting louder and louder, like some mad, laughing cow. It didn't dawn on me, that it was coming from me. I could see Elie's face, his eyes knowing that something was wrong. Then Elie was shaking me and shouting 'Toni, are you ok, what's happened?' I didn't even feel him taking the phone from me, and Elie talking to Sam.

It was only afterwards that Elie told me what I was like that day.

Then I heard Elie say, 'When is the funeral?'

That was when I realised its me that was making the laughing cow noises that I could hear. I then stopped laughing and started shouting at poor Elie. 'It's a lie, she's done this crap before, she ain't dead, I don't believe it.'.

Elie took hours that night trying to convince me that it was true and that the funeral was fixed for Thursday. You know, even with still disbelieving Elie, I phoned back Sam. I was quite calm and I remember barking at him, 'Give me the hospital number, ward and the name of the person who told you this crap.'

I needed to hear it for myself.

Only then, once I had spoken to the nurse and had been told that she, my mother, if you could call her that, was really gone, did I smile, not laughing madly like I had just done, but I had this huge big smile on my face.

I stood up and went over to Elie, who was looking at me quite intensely. I would say now looking back, that he had a slight look of fear in his eyes. I put my arms around him, and held him close, I then told him that it was over, that I can truly be me now, for the first time in my life I felt free.

Poor Elie. I'm sure he thought that I'd gone totally mad, I could tell by the way he was looking at me. But I could also see his love for me there in his eyes, alongside his fear at what had just happened. This was new for him to see, the emotion that I had just shown in these few hours. As you see, my family was a no go area, a subject that I never spoke about to him. Yes he knew who my family was but that was at far as we went into it. I knew that he wanted me to talk about the past and why I had reacted like that, but he also knew I wouldn't.

And Elie, if only you knew, I often think, maybe, that was when I first started to push you away, as if I'd shown you too much of me. I could never talk about my past, and I was too scared to do so again. But maybe, if I had just opened up and talked to you, we would still have been together now.

Through A Seven Year Old's Window 1

H

The secondary school
Where I would go to
The park
Where me and my friends played
The BMX track
Where we went with our bikes
The marshes
Where we went to look
For ladybirds and tadpoles
The housing estate
Where my best friend lived
The car
That my dad drove to work
The winding path
Round the park
Where in winter
We jumped in puddles

Sixteen
TP

It was a few weeks before my sixteenth birthday, and I was getting anxious at what I was going to do when I turned sixteen. Or where I was going to go for that matter. That was when I was going to have to leave the children's home I had lived in for past two years: the only home I knew.

Thankfully my prayers were answered. A lad called Darren who had been in the children's home with me came to see me and he just shocked me by asking me to marry him. No romance just a question.

We had both got on well when we lived in the home but were never an item. He had his reasons for asking me to marry him. You see, we had both had it tough growing up and knew it was going to be hard to move on in life, and even harder to trust someone enough to tell your past to, never mind fall in love, not with the scars we had.

Darren and I shared enough secrets from the abuse and more, that we had suffered, and trusted each other enough to keep them safe, like an unspoken rule not to speak about it all.

He had left the children's home a year before he had come back to see me, and went into the army cadets. But now he was old enough to join up fully and was going to get his first posting. I knew he was scared and worried, as I knew he had been given a hard time in the army cadets because of his upbringing and past. He took a lot of flak over it; to the point he was forever fighting and trying to save face. He was also worried it would be the same in his new posting.

This is some 20 years ago, and at that time it was tough starting up in the army. You had to act as a hard man or take what was being dished out at you. Darren had had his fair share of being used as a punch bag growing up and he wanted it to stop. But it wasn't as easy as that.

One of the lads he did get on well with, told him that if he was married before being posted, he wouldn't have to live in the single squads accommodation and he would be given a house in the married living quarters. Also you were given more respect from the senior commanders. You would be seen to be more responsible, and want to knuckle down and move up the ranks quicker.

So Darren came and asked me to marry him for those reasons. He said to me 'Toni, it would be a way from you escaping from here and at least you would get away from your past.' We didn't love each other and to be honest never have, but I jumped at the chance of a new life.

A few months later just after my 16th birthday we got married. I wasn't prepared for the shock of moving from one institution for another, and nor was I prepared for married life.. It was a hell of a learning curve, and not all that easy either. It didn't end in a happily ever after. Nothing ever does in my life that's for sure, but I'm not bitter. Nor would I change any of my life after I left the children's home, as it is who I am today and part of our 5 children's life past also.

So that was my journey from leaving a past full of secrets never to be spoken out loud, but one I was happy to leave and go into a whole new experience with Darren, but that is another story completely.

Meds Queue: Liars and Secreters

VR

I stand in line for my meds
Where the officers watch you like a hawk
But never catch those who impose
And jump the queue
Thinking they deserve their meds
Before you

Hearing them complain
My leg this, my head that
People blag their way to the front
Saying so-and so saved my spot

At the end of the day
I was there first, but
They don't care, cause most of them
Switch meds with each other

I get to the gate and take my meds
Then finally get away
From that queue
Of liars and secreters

But some or them are still there
Who were there before you
Because they are too nice
And let people pass

Queenie and The Water Man

Queenie's life goes into a downward spiral when she sees the fantastic Water Man

Short Story

WR

Queenie Pickering's hat was always cocked at a cheeky angle. She was very particular about her appearance and was extravagant with her perfume: her favourites were Rive Gauche and J'Adore, a gift from her niece, Janine who was a flight attendant. Janine kept her auntie supplied with perfume and with liquor for her glass-fronted cocktail cabinet with the let-down shelf. The interior light - such an innovation when Queenie bought it in the Sixties - did not work now, and the mirrors and glass shelves were rarely dusted. But it was her pride and joy.

The first time this very unfortunate thing happened Queenie committed herself voluntarily to hospital; she praised the nurses and psychiatrists for their close care, despite her stifled resentment at their calling her Queenie, and not Miss Pickering. Her father's cousin Ralph had been the first one to call her 'Queenie' at the age of six, when she was made May Queen at the carnival in her village. It was Ralph's son who took her to the pictures before he was posted to North Africa to fight Germans. Her father looked down on Tom because his cousin Ralph was a miner and was part of the world he thought he had left behind when he became a professional man. But Tom had liked her, loved her name. 'Queenie by name, queen of my heart.' He wrote that in his very last letter, sent before he was blown up in the sands of Africa..

As she got older only Janine and two or three old friends called her Queenie. Everyone else in her world called her Miss Pickering. Two generations of schoolchildren in her village had called her Miss Pickering. Even when two of her pupils, (grown up now and equipped with mobile phones and Ford Escorts), came upon her one midnight walking through the woodland clad only in her petticoat and armour-like brassiére, muttering lines from the poet John Clare - even these two likely lads called her Miss Pickering.

These young men's kindness and evident distress made

Queenie, that first time, decide she must seek help at the hospital herself. In the hospital the doctor gave her some pills so that when she got back home she no longer saw the Water Man rising, dripping pondweed and silvery fish, fairies dancing at his shoulder. And she missed him, this Water Man who smelled of almonds and honey wine.

After a long while, at the end of a particularly drab day, she decided to leave the pills in their bottle 'just for a day or so'. Then she breathed out, walked around and waited for the sparkle to come back in her life: she waited for the Water Man to arrive again. She put on her hat at its cocky angle, splashed herself with J'Adore and set forth down her garden path.

As she put one foot before the other she started to smile broadly. The colours today were brighter and the noises were louder. People swept by her in warm wafts of light. The buses roared and took on the aspects of scarlet tigers. The cars became insects, bright as jewels.

She exclaimed and laughed at all this beauty. People on the pavement gave her a wide berth. She began walk further and further afield, to drink in all the beauty and allow the Great Ones to come to her - especially the Water Man, her favourite. As the days past she began to return to her little house later and later. Even then, she would be just about ready to get into bed and the beauty of the world outside would call her and she just had to get up and go out again, to bathe in its dark luminescence.

One night she was actually in bed when some lines from Browning popped into her head.

'Thou, Soul, explorest -
Though in a trembling rapture - space
Immeasurable! Shrubs, turned trees,
Trees that touch heaven, support its frieze
Studded with moon and sun and star.'

She chanted the words again and again, racing through her back door and out through a space in her wicket fence towards the woodland. 'Trees that touch Heaven ... Trees that touch Heaven', she shouted out loud. She put up both her arms to join the trees in their touching.

The same young men, Ali Smith and George Onyatt, returning from a late drink at The Green Tree, saw her figure before them, fluttering in a long nightdress, hands waving. 'There she goes again, Ali!' George Onyatt gave chase and soon caught up with her. 'Come on, Queenie,' he said, his voice reasonable. 'This is no way to go on. No way at all.' He grabbed her arm.

She lifted her other hand and whammed him with her fist. 'Miss Pickering to you George Onyatt! Miss Pickering to you and to your father as well.'

He caught her hand in his. 'Come on, Queenie,' he mocked. 'Queenie's good enough for an old loony like you.'

That was when she brought his hand to her mouth and bit it, sinking her teeth to the bone. Howling like a hurt dog, he let her go and slipped to the floor.

She stood still before him, then looked up at Ali Smith who had caught up with them. 'My name is Miss Pickering,' she said. 'You know that, don't you Alister?'

'Yes, Miss Pickering,' he said, taking her hand. 'So it is.'

That time she was taken into the hospital under a section and they gave her the pills that again took away her visions of the giant trees and stars and her Water Man. She was a meek, very good patient. She helped with the tea rounds, taught a young girl to read, and she stayed tucked up in her bed all night, every night.

Her niece Janine visited her in hospital with a grey-suited solicitor in tow. That day Queenie signed over all her affairs into her niece's capable hands. The hospital held a case meeting for Queenie. She recognised the chairman Len Crawshaw, who had once been a very average pupil in her Scholarship Class. It was obvious to all present that Queenie was a prime candidate for Care in the Community - now not only fashionable but compulsory, as hospitals were being closed. When the case committee checked her situation they found that her little house with its cocktail cabinet had been sold by her niece, who had gone off to build a new life for herself and her boyfriend Roger, in the depths of Canada.

But still they found her sheltered housing with a very kind warden. Queenie - for everyone called her Queenie now - Queenie could live there and the nurse could call every week to see that she was taking her medication. Everything would be Hunky Dory. Wasn't that how Care in the Community worked?

At the end of her first week Queenie walked out of the sheltered accommodation, She put on her hat - not so smart now – packed all her most precious things, (including a nearly full bottle of Rive Gauche), into three carrier bags. Then she caught the long distance bus to the town where they would not find her. Best to lie low, she thought. Best to lie low. The gleaming Water Man would be there she was sure. He was everywhere, so he could be in the city as well as the country. And the sky in the city would be studded with moon and sun and stars. And the trees would stride the green reaches in the park..

'There we are, Queenie!' The pale faced girl smiled brightly as she ladled soup into the mug clasped in the old woman's faintly grimy hands. 'Buns at the end of the table, look.'

'Thank you. Kind of you, dear.'

The voluntary helper, (a pale, kind girl who was doing this a month before she went off to help build a school in Africa), watched the old woman in three coats waddled away to her accustomed place at the end of the table. Old woman? Maybe. You never knew how old these people were.

The brisk woman who had showed the girl the ropes here had said, 'Guess how old they look, dear, then take off twenty years.' That should make this old bird no more than sixty-five. Shame. The girl smiled brightly at the next customer, a young man who by that same formula must be no more than ten.

Queenie relished the soup and the thick bread. She had to dip the bread in the soup these days, as she was having trouble with two of her teeth on the right side. Terrible pains, she had. So much so today, hungry as she was, there were thick knuckles of bread which she couldn't tackle.

'Not want those, missis?' The young man who had followed her in the queue was sitting opposite her, slurping his soup. He nodded towards her rejected bread.

'No. No. Can't manage it dear. Teeth, you know!'

'Givin' you gyp, are they?'

Queenie's pushed the hard lumps towards him and let her gaze wander away over his shoulder. She had to keep an eye on her bags, stacked carefully in the corner. She'd had her bags stolen once by some Scallywag and that caused her real heartache. She lost the last of her perfume. That time, in the face of her savage rage, the authorities had made her go into a supervised shelter for a week. Of course they reached for the pill bottle again, and those hypodermics. So she had run off from there as well, taking with her a couple of their own Sainsbury carriers, stuffing them with a few things that were lying around. You never know when they'd come in useful. A brush. A bottle of ink. Some pillowcases. Two old cardigans. Some climbing socks.

Now she looked longingly into the bottom of her cup.

'More soup?' The kind girl was beside her, a white enamel jug in her hand, like a Greek maiden on a vase.

Queenie nodded and held up her cup like a child.

'And was there something wrong with the bread?' The girl looked suspiciously at the man who was chewing away at the tough crusts.

'She give it to us,' he said defensively. 'She give it to us cause her teeth are giving her gyp.'

Queenie nodded. 'Back right, dear,' she said briefly. 'Don't know how it's happened. Always had perfect teeth. My father had his own teeth till he died, you know. Eighty-nine. Born when Victoria was on the throne.' She slurped the soup. 'But then, he knew teeth.'

'Did he?' said the girl. 'He knew teeth?'

Queenie nodded. 'Dentist,' she said.

'A dentist?' The girl's glance became brighter. 'There's a dentist here, Queenie. Calls here on Thursdays. He'll have a look at them. At your teeth. Stop them hurting.'

Queenie placed her cup on the stained bench and shook her head. 'No thank you dear. They'll take me inside. Lock me up again, like they did when I lost my bags. Pumping you full of rubbish.'

'Liquid coshes. That's what they use', said the young man. 'Use them in jail too. Ask anybody. Any more soup for me?' He put his mug under the girl's nose.

'Yes, good name that.' said Queenie. 'Liquid cosh. Dulls you down so you can't live any more, or see things.' She paused. 'Things you want to see, that is.'

'No! No, Queenie,' said the girl eagerly, 'It's not like that. They don't want you to ...'

Queenie tied her third scarf round her neck, and her second scarf round her old hat. She fixed the girl with a look that had frozen many a child in her Junior Three. 'Well, dear, you weren't there, were you?'

'Look!' said the girl desperately, 'They just take a look at you here, in that room back there. Then they can give you something to take the pain away. If you need any more than that, they can take you off to the surgery there and then, or make an appointment…'

'Surgery,' said Queenie, shaking her head. 'No surgery.'

'Whisky,' said the man. 'That's the best thing for toothache. They should give you whisky.'

The girl looked from one derelict to the other. It was not that you wanted gratitude. Sometimes all you wanted them to do was listen to you. She turned away, then turned back. 'Thursdays. This man comes on Thursdays, Queenie, between ten and eleven. Come!'

'Whisky,' said the man. 'That's best.'

Queenie stood up and poked around inside her bags, checking the items to make sure nobody had stolen them while she was talking to that pushy girl. They taught them nothing nowadays. No restraint. No manners. She was pleased she'd had no children. Nothing but trouble. Children.

When Thursday came round Queenie had quite forgotten the conversation with the girl. So she was surprised when, on that day, the girl brought a young man in an anorak and trainers to her end of the table.

'Queenie,' she said brightly. 'This is Jimmy O'Brien. He's a dentist and he could help you with that aching tooth of yours.'

'Dentist?' Queenie surveyed him from head to toe. 'He's not a dentist.'

The young man smiled a perfect-toothed smile. 'Now, what makes you say that, Queenie?'

'Well, first, you're dressed like a ploughman, and second, if you were a dentist you would call me by my right name. You'd have better manners.'

He slid onto the bench beside her. 'So what is your name?' She could smell a sickly smell of violets, mixed with lemon. Men smelling like women! A queer state of things. She moved to the very edge of the bench. 'Miss Pickering,' she said. 'That's my name.'

'Miss Pickering? Well, Miss Pickering,' he surveyed his smooth fingers, his perfectly manicured nails. 'All I'm asking is that we go across to that little room there and you let me take a look at your mouth. Is it hurting now?'

'Yes,' she said reluctantly. 'Like that chap said. It's giving me gyp.

Especially at night. With the cold.'

The dentist and the girl exchanged glances. Nights under bridges or in shop doorways would make anybody's teeth ache.

The girl coughed. 'Queenie ... Miss Pickering, she was telling me her father was a dentist, Jimmy.'

'Is that so? Well, Miss Pickering, he'd have told you that they shouldn't be neglected. Teeth.'

Queenie stirred. 'Well. No harm in letting you take a look-see, I suppose.' Take a look-see. She hadn't heard that for years. She had never even said it herself. That was how her father used to jolly up his patients.

The other two exchanged glances.

'I wouldn't have gone to him, of course.' Queenie announced suddenly.

'Who?'

'My father.'

'Why not?' The young dentist was interested.

'He was never happier than taking the whole lot out and planting in a false set. He had a tidy mind, do you see? But it wasn't fair. Not fair at all. Some good teeth went into his bin. Some very fine teeth. My mother's teeth. They went in his bin too. She never forgave him! He made her into an old woman in a morning.'

A frown marred the boy's brow. 'They did do that at one time. It would never be allowed now.'

'Well, consider him. Died in his eighties with a mouthful of teeth. Only three extractions. Not fair.' She paused. 'Mrs Do As You Would Be Done By!' she said suddenly.

'What?' Now he was entirely lost.

'She's in The Water Babies. Charles Dickens. The children in my class loved it. Mrs Do As You Would Be Done By. If he pulled out all their teeth he should have had that done to him. D'you see?'

'Well, Miss Pickering. As I say, we never take them all out now We move heaven and earth to keep what's there, right in your mouth. I promise.'

Queenie got up, and reached for her bags. 'Very well. You can take a look-see.' And then, she fixed him with a severe glance. 'We'll see.'

In the little room was a dentist's chair of the more portable kind. The boy pulled on his rubber gloves and fixed a disposable bib over Miss Pickering's scarves. He talked to her all the time, concerned that if he left a gap in the talk, she would fly away from under his hand.He took a look at her mouth, this way, that way. His hands were gentle. Then he stood back. 'Look, Miss Pickering, would you like to get this over with now?'

'Over?' She was having problems, from her prone position, keeping her eye on her bags, which the girl had put in the corner.

'There are two in here which look a bit of a ... look a bit poorly and need extracting. And one other which we might manage to save... If you come with me now...'

'Come with you?' She sat up straight. Her bags were still safe. 'Come with you? You might be Jack the Ripper. They said he was really a dentist.' She bustled past the girl and retrieved her bags. 'Or was it a doctor?'

'Janette here will come with us. You know Janette, don't you?'

'She has to give out the soup. She has a job.'

'They've let her off for a couple of hours. So she can help you.'

Queenie pulled her hat down. 'Very kind of them I'm sure.'

'Will you come?' For the first time there was an edge to his voice. 'Will you come, for your own sake?'

She shrugged. 'Well, dear, if it means so much to you.'

Her face felt odd after he had taken the teeth out, as though only her eyes and her nose belonged to her and beneath them was a great yawning gap. And she was slavering! She only realised that when the slaver dropped on to her coat. She couldn't even feel herself slavering. What were things coming to? One by one she smoothed out her scarves and tied them round her neck in the special way she had.The girl tried to help; tried to place her hat on her head. Queenie shook off the girl's hand. 'I can manage dear.'

It was all very strange but it was good to be without the pain.

'Now what shall we do with you?' said the girl called Janette, a bright, satisfied smile on her face.

'What shall you do with me? You? With me?' But the furious words which came out of her mouth were mumbled. She herself could not even understand what she said.

Janette and the dentist exchanged glances.

'Now, Miss Pickering,' said the boy dentist, taking off his rubber gloves. 'You need to be very careful, just for a little time. A day, two at the most. Just so no cold gets into that jaw. Just till that local wears off. So we have a bed in the ward here...'

She mumbled again. 'No. No bed.'

'I know you don't like it, but I promise, promise you that you'll be out in a day, two at the most.' The girl looked quite desperate.

Promises. Piecrusts. She looked at the earnest young face above her. The child meant it. Meant it of course. She did mean to be kind. But she didn't realise. She didn't know what they did with you, once they got you in there. They took your bags away and put them in the incinerator. They inveigled you into a bath. They couldn't wait to wash the smells of the street out of your hair. Then they got out their rattling bottles.

Still, Queenie meekly allowed Janette to settle her comfortably in the waiting room while she went off to sign some forms or other for the dentist. Then Queenie stood up and crept, with only the barest rustle of her bags, out of the room, out of the building; she was down one of her favourite and familiar back streets before the ink was dry on the dentist's form.

There was this little park in the centre of a web of streets: a mere strip of green. But she knew the Water Man would be waiting for her. He was always there at one forty five. Every day. Never missed. They had a long term arrangement. He'd be there waiting for her, smelling of almonds and honey wine.

A Summer Evening Meal

A

She was in the dining room of her home. She could smell the sweet savour of chopped tomatoes, onions and mushrooms and the bad smell of corned beef, She never liked the smell of the toast but when her mum put it in with the bolognaise sauce, she couldn't get enough of it.

She loved cooking with her mum and sitting at the dining table on a warm summer's evening with the patio doors wide open; her brother and and sisters winding each other up. Dad sitting with half a glass of whisky and lemonade with mum beside him with a glass of wine. And them all coming together to eat and talk as a family and it not be like a day at the zoo.

Through A Seven Year Old's Window 2

L

Kids swinging from branches
And breaking trees
Kids throwing stones
At derelict houses
Just for fun
Those lads who robbed cars
Burning them out
Kids getting wood from building sites
And making ramps
This van going on the site at night
To steal from it
I see different people
Day in day out
Smoking heroin on the block.

Through A Seven Year Old's Window 3

C

Flats
With broken windows all boarded up
Mobile shop
Where people go for groceries
Main road
With cars screeching up and down
Pavements
All broken and uneven
And us playing marbles
Poles
To stop cars going up the street
Railings
Around the flats
To stop kids getting in
Trees
All blowing,
Their leaves flying all over
The council place
Where people go
To deal with repairs

Through A Seven Year Old's Window 4

M

The houses across the road
Were terraced like ours
The cars on the street
Were old fashioned
The eight children
Were playing arrows
Split into two teams
I walked out of the front door
To Mr Finlay who was shouting
At the children playing
The little white husky dog
Was always clean and fluffy
The three wheeler bike against the wall
Belonged to my friend next door

Through A Seven Year Old's Window 5

CD

Tree. Along the street it's getting late at night and the street lamps are on. It makes the trees look spooky as if their branches were arms trying to wave to me. Older kids are playing in the street, shouting and you can tell they are pissed. There are cars coming up and down the street, some very fast, doing handbrakes in the street. Sirens now in the back and they chase the fast car.

The chase is on. The lad who is driving the car is only twelve but thinks he's the bees' knees. He crashes the car and his friend comes flying straight through the window. He's dead, all twisted up. I'm crying and shaking now, telling my Mam.

Now there are more police and an ambulance and a fire engine because the car is starting to show flames under the bonnet. Loads of people are running into the street to see what's happening, being nebbie. I'm too young to go out but I know my best friend's brother is dead and the other lad is stuck in the car.

This night has been the worst thing I've ever heard of.

The big question is, what life throws at you.

I'm scared.

Laughing out Loud

Waiting for retribution.

NR

One day the year Amelia was thirteen she got home from school at 3.45pm as usual she had to stop to take her tights off before she got home. It was a Wednesday and her dad comes home from work early on a Wednesday and he hates Amelia wearing tights. A few times Amelia has learned what would happen if she got caught wearing them. She had no idea why her dad hated her wearing them so much. But Amelia's nana told her not to stop wearing them just to take them off before she got home. As she reached her home she saw her dad was filling his van with red diesel he greeted Amelia with his usual request, 'Hold this! Or do that!'

Amelia hated helping fill the van up because it always made her hands stink and it was so hard to get rid of the smell off her hands, After helping her dad Amelia ran into the house, dumped her bag into the hallway and wondered into the small kitchen looking for her mum, but Josephine was upstairs cleaning Amelia's room as she was terrible at keeping it clean.

Amelia greeted her mum with a thank you as she looked at her room. Josephine asked how it was at school but Amelia said, 'Mark Eckelsly pushed me down some steps but he got in trouble for it'.

Amelia asked her mum could she have curry and chips for her tea but Josephine said, 'I'll make it later as I've got washing to do'

Amelia sat in her room. The room wasn't decorated as you could also see all the cracks in the walls and she had no carpet down either. There was just a red metal bed in her room with a box holding her clothes. On her bed Amelia had her favourite cat and mouse bedding on her bed.

Amelia stood on her bed and looked out of the window at her dad messing with his car. She watched Brittany and Lindsey playing scurbee in the street for about ten minutes before her sister Gemma came bouncing in the room laughing and giggling. Gemma is quite a tall girl with very long dark brown hair and she looked the spitting image of her dad. She is also a daddy's girl and does anything to please him. Gemma carried on laughing and

Amelia asked her, 'What are you laughing about?'

Gemma explained that on the way home from school Michelle slipped into a puddle and kicked muddy water all over her mum Julie. Amelia and Gemma started laughing quite loudly and Mark could hear them from outside. He hated Amelia's laugh and he took a fit and yelled, 'Shut the fuck up!'

Gemma kept laughing while Amelia tried to stop but couldn't. Mark shouted again, 'If you don't shut up I'll come up there and give you what for.'

Amelia stopped laughing and Gemma tried but both of them ended up in fits of laugher again over something completely different.

Then all of a sudden Mark appeared at the door and he was pretty angry. As he started toward Gemma with clenched fists, Amelia sat there and watched him lay into Gemma punching her and twisted her arm till she screamed. As Amelia sat there waiting for her turn he finally stopped hitting Gemma and picked Amelia up by the hair and hit her lots of times around the head and in the face until she started to cry and then he stopped.

As he left the room he yelled, 'Anymore of your messing about and you'll know about it!'

Amelia just sat there crying while Gemma got up and ran into her own room as she never shows anyone that she cries. Amelia just sat there crying till her mum come upstairs to find her and she saw Amelia was crying and wanted to know why.

Amelia told her mum that they were just laughing.

Her mum said, 'You know what he's like if he's not happy nobody else is allowed to be'

Josephine told Amelia to stop crying because he'll be going out in a couple of hours and then we'll get KFC.

Amelia cheered up as she liked KFC and her mum asked her to help with the washing as it needed to be brought in from outside.

An hour later Mark came in shouting and raving so Amelia cleared out of the way but Mark shouted her back. He told her that he wanted a bath running, to find him some socks and underwear and tell her mum to iron my shirt and pants. Amelia jumped to do everything he said without moaning because she thought the quicker she does it the sooner he'll go out. While the bath was running Mark shouted Amelia to make him a pot noodle with six buttered slices of bread.

When everything was done he finally got in the bath and when he was done he shouted for a towel. Gemma took a towel up to him and as he got dry Amelia was told to take his clean clothes up to him. As he got ready to go out he told Gemma to ' keep an eye on Amelia and if she causes any shit for your mum you just tell me'. Amelia just looked at Mark in disgust while he winked at Gemma and walked out the front door.

Amelia waited ten minutes before asking her mum about KFC as she wanted to make sure he was definitely gone. Josephine told Amelia she could go get KFC at 9pm when Kelly and Katie had gone to bed.

Amelia waited till nine while helping her mum with the clothes. She tried to put all the socks in pairs which was a hard job to do. Nine o clock came and Amelia got herself ready and asked her mum for the money, Josephine went and got it out of her coat pocket.

Amelia went down to Ince bar where the KFC was and she went in and ordered a bargain bucket like her mum told her too.

As she walked back home Amelia sneaked two chips out of the packet without telling anyone.

She got home and her mum dished the tea out between the three of them. After they had eaten it was Amelia's job to get rid of any evidence, so she collected all the rubbish and chicken bones and walked down the street and put in Chris Kelly's bin which was three houses down.

For the rest of the night Josephine did the washing, Gemma went to bed at ten thirty and Amelia just played on the computer and talked to her mum until twelve thirty. When she heard the car pull up on the front of the house. Amelia dashed off the computer and ran to her room as fast as she could and got in bed. Amelia was used to doing this because her mum liked the company while Mark went out.

She lay in her bed with her plug-in night light on as she couldn't have a big light on because Mark ripped the sockets out the ceiling.

Amelia lay in her bed listening to her dad enter the house and slam the front door and she knew instantly that he wasn't in a good mood. She could hear him demanding her mum to butter him six breads. Amelia could also hear her mum go into the kitchen and

Mark shouting 'How have the kids been?'

Josephine told him that they have been fine. Every thing went quiet for a while as Mark ate his donner kebab, cheese pies and chips from the chippy. Amelia started to drift off to sleep when she heard someone coming upstairs. Amelia tightened her eyes shut while hoping it was just her mum bringing the washing up but she was wrong. It was Mark. First he stopped at the bathroom and went to the toilet, Amelia kept her eyes tight shut praying he wouldn't come to her room. Amelia could hear the creaking coming closer and closer to her room and then she heard her door open. Amelia started to shake a little as he come close to her bed Amelia got Cared as he yelled down her ear ' I know your awake you little bastard'

Amelia tried not to open her eyes but it was too late. Her eyes had opened by themselves. She saw that her dad was completely naked. Amelia just lay there as he stood over her.

Mark told her to get out of bed and get down stairs. Amelia jumped to do what he said and went downstairs, Amelia was quite scared now and nearly wanted to cry because she didn't know what she had done wrong.

Mark grabbed her by the arm when they reached the bottom of the stairs and dragged Amelia to his bedroom and shouted at Amelia, 'I know you've been in here and I want my remote found and the bed making.

Amelia stated that she hadn't been in his room all day, that Kelly and Katie were watching television in the bedroom. Mark out the blue smacked Amelia round the head and pushed her into the bedroom. Amelia began to cry and Mark yelled at her to stop fucking crying and find that remote. Amelia started to look for the remote in all the obvious places but had no joy in finding it and Mark started to get frustrated and yelled at Amelia saying that she wasn't looking good enough, that she was doing it on purpose to annoy him.

Mark shouted Josephine to come in and he asked her does she know were the remote is. Josephine said to ask Kelly and Katie in the morning. Mark demanded Amelia to go wake up Kelly and Katie but Josephine said 'No they have school in the morning and so does she so you'll have to do without it'

Mark got up from the unmade bed and grabbed Josephine by the throat and pinned her against the shoe closet and yelled in her face, 'What I say goes and you never tell me what to do'

Amelia shouted to him to let her mum go but then he grabbed hold of Amelia and hit her repeatedly while yelling, 'No one tells me what to do.'

Mark kept hitting her and her mum walked away crying as Mark finally let go of Amelia and told her to 'get out of my fucking face'

Mark got in his bed and Amelia went to check on her mum. Both of them asked each other if they were OK and Amelia hugged her mum. But Josephine didn't hug back. She just told Amelia it's very late, that she has school in the morning that she better go to bed. So off Amelia went to bed.

Writing In Jail

S

When I came into prison I wanted to send a poem to my partner to let him know I was thinking of him and my family. I looked round the library but couldn't find any which suited how I was feeling. I decided to write my own poem and found that words simply spilled onto the paper.

After being here six weeks I now have a varied collection of my own poems which are going into my own little book. Not that I want any kind of souvenirs of my time in prison but this book represents a period in my life. It is also a collection of my thoughts and the feelings I have gone through over this time.

The poems are in order from the first ones I wrote at the beginning of my sentence and through to the end. The beginning has poems that show the love I have for my family members, my mum, my daughter and my family members. In the middle are poems portraying confusion and anger about the status of my (soon to be ex…) partner. Then the last few are poems to friends and family.

I found that writing these poems down on paper relieved the stress and anger I was feeling. I also felt proud to have produced an end product which made me feel happy in myself, like I'd achieved something for myself.

In Jamaica

SH

I remember the time I was living in Jamaica with my grandmother and the good time we all have together when I was growing up. I look up at the blue skies and the sunset is the most beautiful. And I remember lots of moonlight and the green grass and the trees. At that time my grandmother said to me, 'Shirley you must remember this all your life.'

My grandmother had three children, two girls and one boy, who is my father. And she had thirty-six grandchildren and over sixty-five great grandchildren. She lived to the age of ninety eight years. She died in Jamaica in 2004.

I love my grandmother so much. She is a very beautiful woman. She lives in the parish of St Thomas in a little district called Middleton. My Grandmother was queen of the district. Everyone there loves my grandmother. She is the oldest woman in the district. She was the best dancer, the queen of the comminer[2] dances in the district. The comminer dance is one of the old dances from Jamaica and Africa. The comminer group has four people who play the drums, and men and women and children dance and sing.

Sometimes we go on TV in Jamaica. My grandmother danced for the Prime Minister of Jamaica. Edward Siago.

One day when I was in Jamaica it was a cold and rainy day. But still my grandmother said I had to go to school.

I said, 'Grandma I don't want to go to school this morning.'

She said, 'Shirley you are not staying home from school. You have to go to school so help me God!'

So I put on my uniform and then started to cry.

Then my grandmother asked me, 'Why don't you want to go to school?'

I said, 'It's because I am afraid of the teacher. He is very mean to me. I am trying to be a good student for him but he doesn't like me.'

Then my grandmother said, 'Finish putting on your uniform and let's go.'

[2] *Comminer is a name for a dance with drums on Jamaica*

Then we went to the school and she called on Mr Williams 'Please come here sir. I want to have a talk with you.'

Mr Williams said, 'What about?'

She said, 'Shirley, sir. Tell me something. Is she keeping your wife with you?'

'Why are you asking this question?'

'Because Shirley said you don't like her and you beat her all the time.'

'No Miss Beckford,' Mr Williams said, 'You are living in the past not the present. I am just trying to make Shirley a better person.'

'How do you mean make Shirley a better person? Do you think beating her will make her a better person?'

Then my grandmother and I went back home and she made me my lunch to eat. She made me roast breadfruit and akkee and salt-fish. She said, 'Shirley eat up your lunch because you are going back to school.'

So I ate up my lunch and went back to school.

My grandmother was a very good woman. She love to see everybody happy. On Sunday night me and my friends all go to church and we all sing and clap our hands and dance and pray to the Lord.

That was our lifestyle in Jamaica when I was young and growing up. Such moments were the life in our church. We talked constantly about this and our love of God.

Mr Chalk and Mr Cheese

Two very different people?

Short Story

AMG

Simon was new to the village. He had leased the old barn that had been expensively converted to a superior residence, whilst still retaining its outward character in keeping with the surroundings of the countryside.

Although he was the newest resident, he was a man who seemed to blend in, and was able to mix with the local landowners, farmers and villagers he was equally at ease with commuters and visitors.

Tall, well built, a neatly trimmed beard and eyes that seemed to change colour from grey to green depending on the light. Well dressed, but not ostentatious, his only piece of jewellery, a discreet Rolex on his left wrist. The love of his life was a dark green, soft top Jaguar that was lovingly polished by hand every Saturday morning.

Henry had lived in the village all of his life, born and bred, as were his now dead parents. He had never married, never felt the need to share his cottage or pass on his genes. Henry was always dressed in his uniform of moleskin trousers, battered tweed jacket, with leather elbow patches, and flat cap. He could be seen pedalling his ancient push bike to and from the village pubs on most days, after working on his smallholding where flowers and vegetables grew where they wanted and chickens scratched contentedly, producing enough eggs to provide the village shop with their needs.

The men had exchanged pleasantries over a pint of real ale, and would nod to each other in passing, chalk and cheese to the outsider, what could they possibly have in common, these two very different characters.

Simon woke up screaming, sweat running down his back, his breathing coming fast and shallow, heart pounding. The nightmares were getting worse, more intense and more frequent. Was his dreadful secret catching up with him after all these years? Was he about to be exposed? Paranoia? Obsession? Certainly guilt, he had always had to live with guilt. Mother, forgive me, he whispered aloud into the darkness.

It was such a claggy, uninviting Monday afternoon, Henry's chickens were cosy in their henhouse, he could not work on his beloved garden, so he decided to seek company over a pint or two at the Black Bull. Simon had been working on his computer all morning, not even stopping for lunch. He was determined to finish the report for his client on schedule. At 2pm, he stretched cat like, satisfied with a job well done, slung his leather jacket over his shoulder and headed for the warmth of the bar.

There was only the two of them, a fire was blazing and both men naturally gravitated towards the heat. Mr Chalk and Mr Cheese formed a bond that miserable afternoon. Simon found himself talking about his failed marriages, his estranged children and the many mistakes that he had made. Henry in turn opened up about his thoughts of 'what if', no wife, no children, had he made the right decision in remaining alone or would he grow old and regret it. The men lapsed into silence, each now alone, but in some way comforted by each others presence.

From that afternoon, the bond formed, they would seek out each other on a regular basis an incongruous couple indeed.

Simon's obsession began to dominate not only his dreams, but also his waking day. As his friendship with Henry grew, he asked himself could he at last confide and release himself from his torment, could he trust Henry, or would the confession mean the end of the relationship, or worse? As his agony increased, he decided that he had to unburden himself whatever the consequences. The time was right as this was the first real friend that he had ever known in his life. He chose his time carefully but his well rehearsed speech went out of the window as soon as he started his tale, once he started to speak it just poured out of him.

He was one of twins, born to a couple who had been trying for a baby for years. Although he and his brother were identical, his mother had shown a clear preference for his brother John from day one. In fact she adored John, to the point of neglecting himself, his needs were never considered, all that mattered what was what John wanted. As the boys grew, Simon began to resent John and later, his resentment turned to hatred. John was not only mummy's pet, he was also clever, popular, and good at sport, in fact he was everything that Simon was not. When they were thirteen, the family went on holiday to Menorca, where the boys spent their days swimming and diving on the quiet beaches. On the sixth day, John banged his head on a rock and knocked himself out. Simon raced to his aid, but as he cradled his brother's head, he suddenly thought 'what if I push his head under the water?' that will mean that all the attention will then be given to me, mum will love me as she loves John. Almost without realising what he was doing, he held the face under until no more bubbles surfaced, he pulled the body up the beach and ran for help. It never changed things at all, it made matters worse. His mother was inconsolable and sank into a deep depression, shutting both himself and his father completely, leaving him with only his guilt to dwell on.

Henry was quiet he showed no reaction to what he had just heard. After what seemed an age, he finally spoke. 'Now it is my turn to tell you something Simon'. As you know, I lived with my parents. My father was older than my mother, so by the time I was a grown man he was getting on in years. My father died suddenly from a heart attack ten years ago. He had always been fit and healthy so his death came as a great shock to my mother and just as your mother had, she sank rapidly into depression. Despite tablets from the doctor, it got so bad that she did not want to live and I could not bring any hope into her life. She begged me to help her die by giving her an overdose and staying with her whilst she slipped away, she was too afraid to do it alone. I said no, of course, but she pleaded, she begged, she wore me down until I agreed. I held her hand and tears were silently rolling down my cheeks, as I watched her slip away. I sat with her for hours before calling the ambulance, but of course by then it was too late and she was pronounced dead at the scene.

This time it was Simon who sat there lost for words. The two men had an understanding each had shared their terrible secret. They both knew that it would go no further, would never be referred to again by an unspoken agreement that was made that afternoon and that would last for their lifetimes.

So, Mr Chalk and Mr Cheese were not that different after all.

Waiting (1)

AMG

Worn and weathered moss covered headstones
Stand absorbing the afternoon sunlight
And I wait.

Surrounding me, a welcoming mass
Of nodding blue heads, bluebells in full bloom
Still I wait

The proud chestnut tree stands guard
Like a sentry at his post
Its only purpose is to welcome him
For whom I wait

Sheep calling plaintively in unison
An unheard greeting to him;
As I wait

The old brown bull standing at his gate
Watching my fate unfold
He has seen it all before;
Forever left to wait

Why Do People Pick On Me?

SSC

Why do people pick on me,
I've done nothing wrong,
I just want them to leave me alone,
Until my sentence is done.

The awful names I get called,
Upsets me so, so much,
It hurts I'm in pain,
But there just calling them again and again,

I'm told to hold my head up high,
So high I just want to fly,
But one day I will just crack,
The thing is I don't want to attack.

Anyway I will try to ignore,
The hurtful things they say,
Then just maybe one day,
The pain will go away.

Shirley Talks About Mangoes

SH

You know mangoes grow everywhere in Jamaica. There are about twenty five different kinds of mango – Common Mangoes, Black Mangoes Sweet Mangoes East Indian, Mangoes, Bombay Mangoes. They are sweet and juicy. I miss them. They are yellow, purple looking, green, orange. What we do is wash them and eat them with our fingers, peeling off the skin. You can eat the skin, you know. When they are ripe you can eat them just like that. When they are green they are raw so you can stew them, cook them with meats. When children go on trips to Jamaica they can pick them off the ground because they have dropped the night before. They get juice all over their face, down their chins, on their clothes, and their clothes feel messy and sticky. Mangoes make you full when you are hungry. They make you full of pleasure.

Mirror

NR

Mirror, mirror on the wall
You definitely don't like me at all

Mirror, mirror on the wall
Looking at me with disgust as I stand tall

Mirror, mirror on the wall
Crying and whingeing with no empathy at all

Mirror, mirror on the wall
You're cruel to me for nothing at all

Mirror, mirror on the wall
With one cut you end it all

The Picture

XH

She was drawing a picture. It was a wonderful picture where birds were flying, the sun was shining, and flowers were growing. Her parents labelled her a lover of drawing when she accidentally drew an umbrella on the wall.

She quickly looked round and checked that her mother who was cooking in the kitchen was not looking. She had been a good girl as long as she could remember. She did like drawing but only when she wanted to.

It was just after school, the time for playing with the kids who lived nearby. She wanted to smile and talk with the children who sometimes came over to play. The boys came all the time. The kids were chasing each other and laughing. The little girl wanted to be with them, rather than staring out of the window.

She was jumpy, like ants in a pan. She would shout into the kitchen.

'Mummy, I need some water!'

'Mummy, I need the toilet!'

'Mummy, I'm hungry.'

She wondered why children have to do what they don't like and adults can do what they want. Her little face fell, and her hands stopped moving. Surely all mothers loved their children? Surely her mother loved her? Her mother wanted her to have a bright future, she had been finding a golden path for her. She wouldn't understand till she grew up, maybe until she had achieved her success.

But she desired and deserved her childhood, the playing and laughing with other kids. The window was a hateful thing separating her from her little friends. She went to open the window wider, so she could see everyone outside.

Then, reluctantly, she came back and picked up her pen.

Strange Pathways

Group

Slippyslideypath
Sludgywudgymuddypuddypath
Slimyslipperysquelchingsornfulpath
Froymoysludgyslippingpath
Miftythiftysoftreadingsecretpath
Waterraftingpuddledraftingacquaplaning
- sludgingmudgin path

The Mask

AMG

Can you see me?
No, look carefully behind the mask, where is the real me?
Am I the intelligent, beautiful women that you see?
Or am I the stupid, ugly and unloved creature that I see
Look deeper, where is my passion?
Is it buried deep in my brown eyes?
Is it reflected in my rosy cheeks or perfectly pink lips?
Where you smell Chanel no.5, I smell decay.
You touch hair that feels as smooth as a raven's wing.
I feel tangled wire.

Now can you see me?
Can you look behind the mask?
The enigmatic smile and see what lies beneath?
Well, can you see me?

Tribute

JJ

The siren is like a memory piercing into my night: a warm, rhythmic beat that stings with its sharpness.

I feel in my heart that the world should acknowledge you: all souls should stand and pay tribute to your wonder; they should fall kneeling in your honour, overwhelmed by immense awe

Each memory should be of who you were, and all visualisations, all longings, all grief, sorrow and love should be because of all the things, the very person you could have been; tears and sobbing should echo, carried on the wind

When I close my eyes I am transported back to that room. In the corner the plant stand is empty, the tribute never placed. The rays shining through the window are left to reflect on the varnished wood. Emptiness, desolation fill the room. The air smells cold. The colours dimmed and faded by death. Cream from the walls, shouting that they are still here though you are not. They jeer, announcing that life continues here, But I cannot believe it, cannot feel it. My heart falters. It does not want to beat. It wants to still itself and sleep.

I long for the teasing colours to expand, to spring from the walls and envelop me, I pray for them to entwine me, polluting my being with their toxic joviality.

But no. Instead they remain in place. And the bliss and tranquility, the insanity and detachment I would have in their place elude me.

No flowers scatter where you last lay
And no rosebud marks your final sleep
The only tributes that show your passing
Are the tears I constantly weep.

Where am I going?

A father takes a journey with his daughter.

Short Story

AMG

'Dad, are we nearly at the airport?'

'Not yet pet, why don't you count all the red cars you see until we get there?'

Lucy concentrated hard and pulled on the pigtails that she hated so much as she focused her pale blue eyes on the road ahead.

'Dad, will I be able to go on all the rides when we get to Disneyland?'

'Yes, of course and have your picture taken with Mickey Mouse.'

Lucy digested this information thoughtfully did she really want to get that close to a mouse?

Dad, I need a wee! Lucy announced, just after they had passed a service station. 'Now Dad'.

Mike managed to distract his daughter by telling her an adventure story. At last the airport buildings loomed into view.

'I can see our aeroplane Dad', Lucy squealed.

She was so excited. Mike loved this skinny little girl so much, she was the very image of his dead wife and he always had bitter/sweet feelings when he looked at his precious daughters face. She had only been four when Sarah had died, now she could hardly remember her mum.

They checked in their bags, Lucy quizzing the staff what they were going to do with her favourite patched-up stuffed dog Oscar, whom she had insisted on packing. Mike could not help himself, with tears in his eyes the big man stooped down and gave her a hug.

'Dad, that's not cool.'

Out to the plane, Lucy gazed up at the silver beast – it was ginormous! Was that really going to fly she wondered.

'You sit next to the window Lucy then you can see all the clouds.'

Lucy hoped to see more than clouds, maybe she would see angels, maybe even that special angel that had come for her mummy.

A very pretty lady came and made sure that her belt was

fastened up then she had a funny feeling in her tummy, like when she had gone to the funfair, as they rose up into the sky.

'Are you alright pet?'

For once in her life, Lucy was too excited to speak.

The pretty lady then gave her a tray with all her dinner on it at once, how fab was that, she could eat her pudding first and her dad couldn't stop her because she had already stuffed it into her mouth.

'Time to wake up Lucy', Mike whispered. They were in America.

Welcome to Disneyland!

It was difficult to tell who was more excited, Lucy or Mike. Everything was bigger and brighter than at home in England. All the food came in large or extra-large portions, the Americans had never heard of small. Next day they would explore the magic kingdom, but for today both father and daughter were completely exhausted. Bed was calling.

Mike woke with a start, he looked across at the other bed, and it was empty. Lucy must have got up to go to the loo. He then heard a sobbing, breaking little voice calling Dad. Where was Lucy? What was wrong?

He realised with horror that the voice was coming from OUTSIDE the window! Lucy was on the window ledge, forty storeys up, his stomach went into spasms, he whispered My God, help me.

Lucy wobbled when she saw Mike and nearly lost her footing, how had she managed to get so far along the narrow piece of concrete, now she was too terrified to move. Could he manage to inch his way to her, pick her up, and get back inside safely? No chance, and no way could he leave her now that she had seen him, not even to call for help.

The seconds slowly passed, think man, do something. The sweat ran into his eyes, he dare not wipe it away, no movements, he might distract Lucy. His head pounded, THINK.

Finally, with as much composure as he could manage, he asked Lucy to look at him and to move very slowly sideways towards him, pretend that she was a crab like they had seen in the sea life centre. Nothing happened. Lucy was crying softly, and for the first time since his wife's death, she was calling out for her Mummy. Then slowly, almost as though an unseen hand was holding her, Lucy started moving along the ledge towards the window. Mike held his breath.

Unbelievably, Lucy was smiling! A few more inches, their fingers touched, don't grab her Mike ordered himself, now he had her hand, then her arm – he had all of her. Thank you God, oh, thank you.

Lucy seemed strangely calm, saying that she had not been afraid after her mummy had held her hand and guided her back to daddy. She never mentioned mummy again after that night, or the window incident. It was as though it was completely forgotten. But Mike would never forget, or be able to explain just what happened that night, he would always remember that holiday to Disneyland where things are never what they seem.

The Garden

A

The wind blows ever so slightly among the peaceful garden, which remains empty to those who can not see beyond the weeds and a rusty old forgotten swing.

This once was alive with kids swinging and playing all over it.

Looking back I can see this once so beautiful garden with the pond filled with luscious lily pads floating around the gorgeous pond when the water sparkled under the bright orange sun, but now its so very dull and lack of life and colour.

This once so beautiful habitat is now overtaken by weeds, dead flowers, overgrown grass and a stale pond. The dead tree which rears over the garden was once full of life and energy, its twigs full of green leaves, and apples grew so lovely and birds nested within its heart. But now not a living soul will live again in this particularly tree as it has been neglected, just like the garden.

The wind calms now and everything this was still the garden sleeps away until one day tender hands to help it to be reborn again.

Crack House

A

People shouting who's next on the pipe
People inhaling smoke
A lot of people lying down groaning
I Think I'm Better Than This
Gis a lick of a pipe Will you get us?
Hurry up Babe
A brown old tired out sofa
A lamp that has been used
I love you but I don't like you
People say what are you doing in this dive
I think I am better than this

Friends

SC

I have a friend who listens to me,
She tries to make me smile,
She listens to me when I'm feeling down,
She's good to have around.

I know she's always busy,
And doesn't always have the time,
But when she does we have a laugh,
And I don't feel so daft.

She encouraged me to write my feelings down,
It was really hard to do,
Most of the time I'm lifted up by her words of wisdom,
At this moment in time she's a good friend
In all the kingdom.

But sometime soon I will be leaving here,
And won't ever be returning,
But until that day she will be around,
And I thank her for being so caring.

The Journey

AMG

This was the day that the journey would begin. I had waited all my life for this moment and now instinct told me the time was right. There was no time to lose and many miles to cover if I were to reach my destination in time, my heart quickened a the prospect of what lay ahead: the North Atlantic and then the rivers of Eastern Scotland. With an almighty swish of my tail, I headed east, full of energy, in the very prime of my life, nothing could stop me. I was invincible.

Progress was swift as the current carried me along like a silver torpedo speeding through the greyish green water. My mind was set only on my destination, nothing else mattered, not even eating.

Suddenly, I felt a strange tightening around my body, something cruel was cutting into my skin, restricting all my movements. Next thing I was hauled up through the water and dropped on to hard wooden boards – the deck of a fishing boat. I gasped, drowning in the air that now surrounded me. Rough hands released me from the net and I flapped ungraciously. I thought that I was doomed when a sudden swell rocked the boat and I was thrown to the side and with superfish effort flipped over the gunnels and splashed down into the cool, life-giving water. My skin tingled, but there was no obvious damage, I was one lucky salmon. The journey resumed, I was now even more determined to fulfil my purpose.

I began to taste the difference in the water. Salt gave way to fresh I was at the river mouth, not far to go now, but danger all the way. Now the going really got tough, only mighty leaps of supreme effort would ensure my progress upstream. I was exposed to predators as my silver scales were shimmering in the sunlight like an invitation to dinner.

Exhausted, I finally reached the calm shadows – my destination. With one final effort, I gently scooped out a hollow in the gravel and laid my eggs, my job was done my incredible journey was over.

First Word, Last Word

SSC

Sometimes scared to come out of my room
Unsure if I'm going to face my doom
I'm not sure what could happen next
Can't think what I can do for the best
Isolated I shouldn't have to feel this way
Dreading it when I leave here one day
As they lock my door at night
Listening to my suicidal thoughts ...what a fright

The Need To Light a Torch For Ourselves

XH

There are some people, noble and lofty, living in the world, but I hadn't met one before. Probably then I was in such a hustle and bustle that I didn't notice the blooming flowers and lovely smells. When the father said, 'Let us pray,' we prayed for the whole world. I learned that it wouldn't be enough to pray for myself. He prayed for the people who are suffering from the floods and the hurricane, which I used to worry about but not at this time. We are in prison to serve our sentence, not be on holiday! Where is the spare mind to worry so much about big things? I can't indulge in lengthy and empty talk while my heart is in my throat for my own future. Such tolerance and generosity is hard to attain at this time when people like me are labelled as selfish and squalid and can be blamed and cursed. But I must not vex and grate. Who was it who said, 'We can't hold the torch for others before we light a torch for ourselves?' Perhaps we should be baptised. And perhaps it is bad to be bogged down in details about ourselves. But only to see the big world is worse.

Little Village

NR

In a little village in a town so quiet
Lived a woman whose life was as sad as can be
Every day she watched her husband rotting away
Lazy man who struggles even to put out the trash
Weaker and weaker he walks
Among the crowds of people

These were a really odd couple
Who fought over the window being open or closed.
He visits a dead tree that once lived in his eyes
She looks at the sky so blue and the sun so bright
She wishes so hard and with frightened eyes
That her sad pathetic husband should be dead

A dark black figure strolling along with giant legs
Who was ten feet tall
Put the man out of his misery,
Stood on him and cheered to all
The sad woman smiled with glee
'Now I don't have to clean up after thee.'

Journey Into Life

AP

Cocooned in fluid, eyes shut to the world,
Not yet born as time unfolds,
9 months on and I'm bursting my mother's seams,
I'm ready and waiting, to take my journey of first breath,
As I'm crushed, squeezed, turned and prodded,
I urge forward and slither out into bright lights and blurred faces,
Comforted by my mother's touch and warmth
My journey has begun.

Up And Down

JA

Up and down and
Round and round
I see you looking at me
With a smile on your face

Then you disappeared
Like an angel
Without a trace
Around and around and around

The Tree House

A Children's Story

Extract.

HM

Chapter 1

I am on my way to visit Granddad and Grandma at their new bungalow; I have never been in a bungalow before. It sounded funny that you did not go upstairs to sleep. When I arrived I was really surprised at the size of it and the garden, there were loads of places to play.

The bungalow was very old; it had huge oak beams and a large fireplace in the living room. Grandma explained that is where people in the early 1900s cooked; the large hook for the pan was still there. I really like the place, especially the bedroom for the grandchildren; it had bunk beds, bookcase, chest of drawers with TV and DVD with the video on the top of it plus 3 large toy boxes.

'When we're settled in Jimmy Granddad and I will decorate this room and make it special for all of you' Grandma told me.

I have brothers and sisters, Aiden is 13, Justene 11 and Drake 5, by the way I'm 9 and we all live with my mother Te.

At the moment Drake is in hospital as he has had a second operation on his leg, he is very brave and we all hope he will soon be able to walk a lot better.

Grandma and I then went to look around the garden we came to a very large old oak tree which had no leaves or branches on it which is sad, as all the other trees were full of leaves and blossom.

'Jimmy do you think this would make a super tree-house for all of you'

'Yes grandma but who would make it'

'Granddad of course would build it and I could help fetch and carry things for him and make coffee and cake to keep him going'.

Grandma was a very good cook we had lots of fun in the kitchen baking and cooking with her. She taught us how to measure everything out, mix and bake, then she would let us go off and play of watch TV whilst she tidied up.

When it was our birthdays she would make us a special themed birthday cake. Last year I had a Newcastle United football shirt cake, I support them even though I live in York, I hope to go and see them play one day.

We wandered round to the garage to Granddad. It was large and had room for Grandma's car, Granddad's BMW motorbike, and another BMW which he was renovating. He had seen it in a neighbour's garden and offered to buy it from them. The motorbike had lain in the garden for over a year so was extremely rusty and would not start, Uncle Noel had helped Granddad get it back to their old house. I had watched and helped Granddad over the winter months do work on it. It was now beginning to look like a proper motorbike again.

'Hi, Jimmy what are you doing up here, who brought you up. Mind you it is good to see you'.

'Hi Granddad, mum brought me up. She's gone to the hospital to be with Drake. I like your new house and garden, Grandma says you will make us a tree-house in the big tree'.

'Did she now?' That was good of her, he said laughing. Well we will have to discuss this over coffee. What say you Grandma?'.

'Ok, what would you like to drink Jimmy – I suppose you boys would like some cake as well'.

'Can I have a chocolate milkshake please, and can I help?'

'Of course come in 5 minutes Granddad'

We went off into the kitchen. She made the coffee while I made my milkshake; I put a coffee cake on a plate. It was funny opening cupboard doors and finding things as in the old house I had know where everything was kept.

'Go and get your Granddad please Jimmy'

'Ok Grandma'

'Granddad coffee is ready! Can I stay the night please and be the first to sleep here please, please?'

'Well you will have to ask Grandma but I think we know what she will say don't we?' He said laughing.

I ran back into the house. 'Grandma, can I please, please stay tonight?' I loved staying with them I had spent lots of time with them over the past 9 years. We had such fun and had been to wonderful places.

They supported my rugby league. I played for a local club which was always top of the league. Often grandma would take me my brothers, sisters and cousins to see Leeds Rhinos, the team we all supported. We would go off after tea so we could get a place on wall right, on the pitch side. Poor grandma would have to stand on the terraces. The game didn't start till 8pm so we would sing songs and chat to everyone around us, then Ronnie Rhino the club's mascot would come on to entertain us. Often after the game we would stop at McDonalds for supper. Usually by the time we got to York some of us would be asleep then we would sleep over and have a slob out the next morning.

'Of course you can stay darling, but maybe Aid and Jus will want to say also because I'm picking them up at 4pm. Now where is the old man? 'She said laughing' just one piece of cake'.

I knew Granddad would ask for more. They would have a fun argument with Granddad winning and Grandma shaking her head in laughter.

Chapter 2

We were all sitting round the dining room table. Grandma had found a large piece of paper – the designing of the tree-house had started.

We first came up with some silly ideas, 2 floors with an upstairs bedroom, pool table, flat Screened TV which I thought would be brilliant but Granddad definitely said no to. Grandma said maybe beanbags, toy boxes and if we were good a portable TV/Video if we could put electricity in.

Eventually we came up with a brilliant design, a large base over the tree trunk with supports from the ground, 4 walls it would have 2 windows a door and of course a roof to finish it off.

'Could you really make that Granddad?'

'Yes I should think so, we will have to refine the plans first'.

'What's refine?'

'Well get the exact measurements for everything starting with the supports then work out the base area and from that the rest of the building, this is not something we can rush all building work, works out so good if the plans are correct in the first place, do you understand Jimmy?'

'Yes I think so Granddad'

'Then we have to work out a work plan, shopping list, go talk to Uncle Malc to see if he can put electricity in'.

Uncle Malc was Granddad's best friend and they often did jobs together.

'Can I help please Granddad?'

'Of course you can Jimmy in fact all of you can help'.

'Will you help too, Grandma?'

'I expect I will be the general dogsbody'.

'What's that' I asked laughing.

'Well it is someone who fetches and carries, doing what they are asked and hopefully I'll get involved with the interior, with your help of course Jimmy, isn't that right Granddad'.

'Of course dear that is your forte'.

'What does forte mean grandma?' That's another word I haven't heard before.

'It means something you can do really well, like you do with your rugby'

'Oh I understand now – can I go and play out for a bit now?'

'Thought we were planning a tree-house' exclaimed Granddad 'go on and I'll have another cup of coffee in peace. Would you like your bike out?'.

They had different sizes of bikes so we could all ride our bikes together. Granddad and I went off into the garage to get my bike. He told me to stay in the garden and not to ride on the flowerbeds.

The garden was in 5 sections, as you came round from the front of the house there was a lawned area, then a pretty fence with flowers growing on it, through the gate into a bigger area which led up 2 steps which came into the wild garden where the old oak tree was which soon would be our tree-house. This part was separated by a rockery with big stones. At the side of the large area there was a patio with a summer-house and behind that a vegetable garden and greenhouse.

I was having great fun riding round the garden doing jumps down the steps and finding great hiding places. I realised this would be a fantastic garden for the Easter party.

Every year Granddad and Grandma gave an Easter party. They would hide little presents, all wrapped in different coloured paper, one colour for each child because my 5 cousins would come as well.

First, we would be give a clue to find the first present, on that would be the clue for the next present and so on until we had all 6 presents, and then we would have to put all the clues together to work out where our main present in the house would be.

After the treasure hunt we would paint hard-boiled eggs, tea would follow which was always super. Then Grandma would put us into 2 teams for a quiz so that the adults could have a bit of piece.

Before, we went home we would roll our eggs along the path to see whose went the furthest, gosh it made such a mess poor Granddad had to clear it up whilst Grandma cleaned the house up. All in all great fun was had by all.

'Jimmy where are you, we are going to take measurements for the tree-house, you can help with the measure and Grandma will write down all the measurements.

First we measured the girth of the tree, then the distance from the ground to where the base of the tree-house would be for the supports, then Granddad worked out the height the tree-house would be. When all the measurements were taken we went inside to make a shopping list before we could go to the timber yard and finally a list of the order in which we would do the work, all in all a very productive afternoon.

Grandma then went off to collect Aiden and Justene whilst Granddad and I went to tinker about in the garage.

Chapter 3

As soon as Jus and Aid arrived I showed them around the house and the garden, telling them about the plans for the tree-house. I think Aid was jealous he had not been part of it, but he decided that morning to go to his friends instead of coming here. He became really angry with me and we started fighting. Jus had gone off to help Grandma get tea ready.

'Now you boys that's enough – what is going on?'

'He started it Granddad' I said.

'No you did you little snot it was him Granddad, Jimmy who started it'.

Granddad raised his voice 'I don't care who started it you can both come inside now'

He marched us into the house 'now you can both sit down and when you apologise to each other you can watch TV.

It took us half an hour before we would apologise to each other I don't think either of us wanted to but we wanted to watch TV.

After a great tea of shepherds pie and vegetables followed by my favourite dessert of banana split, a banana split in two with a scoop of chocolate and vanilla ice-cream in the middle and topped off with chocolate sauce, we got ready to visit Drake in the hospital.

On the way we talked about rugby, Jus was not impressed wanting to talk about shopping but Grandma liked rugby too and anyway Jus would often come to watch the games with us at Leeds Rhinos.

'Now Aid and Jus are you sure you do not want to stay with us tonight it is no trouble at all'.

'Thanks Grandma but I would like to go back to Sue's all my school things are there anyway'.

'Ok sweetheart and what about you Aid'.

'I'll go back to Robert's as we still have some homework to do but I would like to come and stay soon please'.

'Of course you know you are always welcome all of you'.

On arrival at the ward Drake came rushing across to us in his wheelchair nearly knocking Granddad over, he looked so much better, I think we were all happy with the positive change in him. Then to hear he was coming home tomorrow although it would be a couple of weeks before he could go back to school.

'Granddad, Grandma look at me in this wheelchair and I can now walk on my frame isn't that good, let me show them mum'.

'Well be careful. No showing off. Hello Aid, Jus, Jimmy have you all had a good day?'

'Sue was moaning because her mum would not let us go to town I thought it was unfair as well,' moaned Jus.

'Well I'm glad,' said mum 'what about you two boys?'

'We went swimming and had a great time thanks mum, you look great Drake lets see you walk,' said Aid.

'Granddad and I are going to build a tree-house, Drake I'm so pleased to see you looking so much better'.

'Hang on young man, I said we could all build a tree-house. Now Drake do you need help out of that mean machine of yours'?

'Yes please Granddad'

You could see Drake was in pain as Granddad helped him out of his wheelchair but he was very brave and we all clapped when he took a few steps.

'Why don't you kids go off into the playroom whilst I chat to

Granddad and Grandma' said mum.

Granddad helped Drake back into his wheelchair and we all went off to play.

The playroom had 2 large game-boys, lots of board games, books, chalkboards with chalks, paper, pens and crayons, soft cushions, slide and toys of all sizes.

Drake and I had a game of football on one of the game-boys whilst Aid played on the other, Jus just had a strop so went back to mum.

After an hour it was time to go, Drake became really upset he wanted to go and stay at Granddads and Grandma's.

'Do not worry sweetheart, I will be here to pick you up in the morning as soon as I have dropped Jimmy off at School. If you feel up to it you and mum can both come back to our house for lunch'.

'Yes, please Grandma, can I have a hug and will you help me back into bed?'

'A hug of course sweetheart, but I think we will let Granddad lift you onto your bed, then I will give you a hug'

A great fuss was made of getting Drake into bed then we all said goodbye and left.

We dropped Aid and Jus off at their friends then on the way home stopped at Uncle Malc and Auntie Ges house. We were greeted at the door by Sasha, their 8 year old German shepherd dog, who made loads of noise but was so gentle, I had grown up with her and Granddad could remember when she was just a ball of fluff who sat in the palm of his hand.

'Uncle Malc, Granddad is going to build a tree-house in the old oak tree and will you put in the electrics please?'

'Well hello to you as well Jimmy, what is this about a tree-house tell me all about it.'

'Well we've drawn up the plans it's going to have a roof, 2 windows and a door, then we made a work plan of jobs to do in the right order, but Granddad can't put the electrics in so could you as you are an electrician.

'Well what would you need the electrics for?'

'Granddad what would we need them for?'

'Oh I thought a light socket and a couple of plugs.'

'Well I cannot see why not, I would have to come round and see where I could feed the electricity from,' said Uncle Malc.

'Great thanks can I go out and play, everyone is in the square'

'Yes but no leaving the square Jimmy' said Grandma.

There was a large square outside all my friends were playing. Granddad and Grandma had lived just two doors away from Uncle Malc before they moved, so that is how I knew everyone.

About an hour later we went home and I was allowed to have a Jacuzzi bath before supper. I had never had a Jacuzzi bath before. The bubbles were great.

After milk and biscuit, Grandma tucked me up in bed. I had spent a brilliant day and had lots of exciting new thing to look forward to. I loved being with Granddad and Grandma feeling safe once again.

Feather, Feather!

NR

Feather, feather bright and colourful
Come on down from your world in the sky
Feather, feather, let me touch your softness
With my delicate hands…
Feather, feather, lower yourself
For just a little minute
Feather, feather, I know you're scared
I won't let anyone hurt you…
Feather, feather, I can see your soft glow
I will not tease or throw you away
Feather, feather, don't be scared of the weather
It's only rain, nothing to fear…
Feather, feather, I'll just hold you
Come on now, don't float away
Feather, feather, I can barely see
Your beautiful glow…
Feather, feather,
Gone forever

The Resurrection

Tuning into a relationship

A Short Story

AMG

I can clearly remember the first time that I met him. The bongs of News at Ten were on the pub TV as I walked in the door and there he was, sitting with my old cronies. As was usual I asked who wanted a drink and included him, he declined. When I sat down, my good friend Ian introduced us.

'Louise this is Chris'

He barely acknowledged me.

I carried on talking about the seminar that I had been to that evening. The old boys enjoyed my company and I enjoyed theirs: their tales of the past when they were young men, the hopes and dreams, some fulfilled, others now lost forever.

After a couple of drinks I left for home, waving an all encompassing hand to the group and I was gone.

Next day, Saturday was our day for meeting up at lunch time for a joint effort to crack the Telegraph crossword. I squeezed my way to my seat through the noisy bar.

'May I join you?' The man called Chris, immaculate in Armani, slipped into the seat beside me. His hazel eyes gleamed in the smoky bar light. 'Can I buy you a drink?' His deep voice, soft and articulate rang in my ears and made me catch my breath.

My interest in the crossword disappeared, I stuttered, 'Thank you, Vodka Tonic please. Beneath the table I could feel my knees go weak. What was this man doing to me?

When he got the drinks we started talking, the noise of the pub subsided and we were now alone. All I could hear was his dark brown voice. Nothing mattered to me except being with this man.

The crossword remained unfinished. My friends had all left for home. I got to my feet, reluctant to leave. Chris sat tight. Then he said 'I've been wondering if you'd like to join me for dinner tonight?'

My heart leapt to my mouth and butterflies played havoc with my stomach. I actually blushed. At my age too! 'Yes' I said. 'Yes I would like that'.

That evening when I arrived at his apartment, the table was set with silver and crisp white linen, the smells of roasting duck and freshly zested orange filled the air. After we had dined, he poured two generous measures of cognac and turned off the lights leaving us in the glow from a single candle. He took my hand, led me to a reclining chair, told me to relax and listen to the music that he had selected, to remain silent until the piece had finished and to concentrate completely on the music.

I had never heard anything like it before, the orchestra building to a crescendo then a massed choir filled the room.

'What was that?'

'Mahler's Second symphony The Resurrection,' he replied. And he took my hand and pressed the CD into it. 'That's to remind you of this evening', he said.

From that night we were inseparable, I could never have imagined in my wildest dreams that two people could have been so close. I would have done anything for this man. After three weeks he asked me to marry him, I accepted. Plans were made, life was wonderful, I had never been happier, I was even promoted at work, life could not have been better.

Then it happened.

Friday, early evening after work, drinks with the crowd as usual, me laughing and relaxing but with one eye on the time, my mind purring with the thought that Chris would be here any minute now, but that Friday he was late.

Another drink, but time was getting on. Try his mobile. Switched off. Now this was strange. I felt uneasy. I decided to go home and start on dinner. There was no need to panic. He was probably caught in the traffic. He would have phoned if there was a problem. Dinner was cold, I was cold, it was now dark and I was still none the wiser as to where he was. At midnight I rang the local hospital, Chris had not been admitted. I then phone the police but they could not do anything as it was too soon for him to be classified as a missing person. What a long, unfriendly night that was, every little creak made me jump, but there was nothing, just nothing.

The days merged in to one another after that. He had disappeared into thin air. His car was in the office car park, no one at work had any idea as to why he had not acted strangely. His bank account remained untouched. Where the hell was he?

Weeks turned into months, the old boys whispered suicide, how could I accept such an idea, we had been so happy. Eventually I settled back into a routine as much as I could, then one Friday afternoon my life changed again.

For some reason, my eye caught the obituary column in the paper.

Chris De Vere, died suddenly, funeral on Wednesday, 3pm, at All Saints Church, Brisley, enquiries to E.G. Loms, Funeral Directors.

With shaking fingers, I dialled the number, hoping that there was another man named Chris De Vere, and that it was he who had passed away, not my Chris. No, the man said. The date of birth confirmed my worst fears. It was My Chris, oh my God.

That night I lay awake. So many unanswered questions swirled in my head.

Brisley was the other side of the country, why had Chris never mentioned his connection to the area. Could it be that his parents were buried there? Why did it matter anyway, all that was important was that I was present at the funeral to say goodbye to my true love. I would make the journey.

It was a quiet funeral apart from the loud music – the music his wife chose was The Resurrection.

Backhouse Avenue West Bank Park

M

Children's Laughter
Bowling balls knocking together
Squeaking of the swing
Gimma the ball, kick it here
Mother push me higher, higher
Oh get off the grass you little Camp
Aww, noo, Mother's gonna kill you
Look at the state you're in
Our Mother saying
Take care because I care
Before we go
The Lodge, the old caretaker's house
Belonged to old James Backhouse
People say the house is haunted
I think it's a load of old cob wash
Old man Backhouse trying
To scare the locals.

Heaven and Hell

XH

The man falls again into unconsciousness. He makes a dramatic effort to lift his eyelids and again he fails. He tries again as he hears his wife murmuring words of love. But he is preoccupied again by one thing that has bothered him for a long time. Is he going to Heaven or Hell after he dies? Nobody knows what is going to happen after that; probably there is no choice. But as long as his brain is alive he wants to make a decision.

It's tough, logically. Heaven is a place everybody longs to go to. It's a place filled with angels and flowers. If a person has lived a moral life he can go. But this man's life is full of immorality: gambling, prostitutes, lovers, drugs. He thinks that without these things, where is the excitement, and attraction of these things? Who is going to play poker with him when he gets to Heaven? He would be bored to death!

He reckons all the good things would be easy come by in there. Then where would he find the feeling of content over conquering to achieve the commodities of life? He wouldn't like that place.

Before he opens his eyes he decides he would like to go to Hell after he dies. That must be an interesting place. You might languish in poverty but you would be there with interesting people – swindlers, gamblers, thieves.

He thinks that even though he'll pay a lot for it, he will taste his life.

Hunstanton (The Promenade)

S

People walking along the beach
The water rushing against the rocks
It's really beautiful
The old pier that was burnt down
Do you have to go out looking like that?
People say this is lovely in summer
I think this is a nice place to love, and live

In My Prison Cell

SH

I can hear the sound of music
I can hear the women talking
I can heat the women in their sleep
Drowning, snoring tonight
The four walls and the fence around us
And my TV and my washroom
The officer calling, saying
Please turn down that music!
People think I am mad

My grandmother used to say
Shirley, if you don't have anything
No clothes, or money
Just remember, have manners
It will take you far

I think we are living in hell.

Doxy

Ch

Love ya lass
Think it's cushy
Doxy MASSIVE!
Music blasting
Laughing and singing
Let's get out if it
Giz a tinnie
Love ya daft lad
Doxy bad boys
I think it's cush
Doxy MASSIVE!

The Visit

XH

I had a visit today – a visit from hundreds of sparrows. They landed on the lawn under my window. They came to deliver the sounds of nature for me. The voice of the natural world passed through my window and arrived by my bed.

I opened my sleepy eyes and jumped to the window, under the delusion that I was still in a dream. The spectrum of the sun cut across the snowy clouds. The glisten of the morning dew reflect into my vision. Some of them flutter their feathers, chasing each other under my window. Some of them settle on the prison fence.

I could hear them chatting about how my world could be delved into. They were so kind neither scorning me nor seeing me in disgrace. They didn't need to fly to me but just be there near me. I knew that not only would they not talk to me; they would not stay with me.

Now they come to visit me sometimes as though visiting my deep heart. How lovely today that they wielded the power of nature to comfort me. They don't know me, much less are they my friends. But they were the complementary friends of my soul.

We are comforted as soon as we can hear the voice of the natural world.

Newton Aycliffe Town Centre

TR

People are passing me
Talking amongst each other
Mum shouting at her child to slow down
Ding dong the Town Hall Clock has just struck
Youngen!
Buerk!
Ding!
Towny!
Smackrat!
Our lad!
Bookys!
Town Clock
Upper Beveridge Way
Nowt there
People say town-shite
I think Aycliffe's home

I Cry Over This Number With No Tears

XH

That's the only number I can remember, but it goes to voicemail straight away.

I have been thinking of millions of excuses for that. Maybe I dialled at the wrong time. Maybe she is in the shower or still sleeping. Or possibly she is working and can't answer the phone. That's how I fool myself to feel better when unwisely I go to the phone box at different times. Still no answer. Even so I was not convinced that the person did not want to answer it. I have never thought that my best friend would walk away without saying goodbye. How could you dump your friend when they are in trouble? Especially one with whom you had a certain parallel community of thought?

I 'm so innocent about people and I am blind with friends.

As the day merges into night my mood sinks to the very bottom. Even if I go to chapel every day in the future I do not feel like forgiving her. Eventually I might forgive her but I will never forget. I am human, not divine.

A man has said, 'We read that we should forgive our enemies, but we don't read that we should forgive our friends.' Because there is no way to forgive due to our ignorance of ways to forgive our friends. Isn't this true?

The number I dialled will never more be dialled. It will fade as the time goes by, as the colour fades from the flower, as the drop merges with the stream. The number will be enfolded by my mind and will never more emerge. I cry over this number with no tears.

I am deaf and dumb at this moment. The TV is on and the people are talking in the film. I have been staring at the screen for twenty minutes but have no clue what it is about. My friends sitting beside me talk to me sometimes but I just simulate interest. The world around me seems to stop. Why can't I hear anything? I am trying to think and work out how they have done this to me. But it's hard, as hard as any exam you can imagine.

I am lying in bed with my brain gone numb, not only because of the number, but because of the person holding this number. The attack is like the fire from a gun that will shoot you dead. You wouldn't believe it would you?

52 Dalviat Road

A

Hamish from a couple of doors down, barking
The seven Cullins shouting at each other
My brother shouting 'Mum!'
I'm away down the pub
Och what have you done this time?
I'll see you later
Balloch (down the road)
I'll skelp your bottom
It's lovely but cold

Places We Meet

Group

In the nightclub
Where I danced
I caught a glimpse
In the glittering light
So handsome and young
The man I dreamed of

In a hospital ward
Where I was ill
I saw a nurse
She was pretty, she was thin
She was the most bountiful thing
As she walked by I caught her eye
I wished she were here with me
Not this doctor
He's a bore!

Under the bridge
Where the water flows
Like a flash of ice
Cold and deep
I wonder why you went away
On that cold winter's day

My Special Visit

SSC

I had a visit from dad today
It wasn't that good, I just wanted to get away
He said my letter really upset him
But he doesn't realise how my life is dim

If he really cared why didn't he answer my letter?
Just to see if I was feeling better
I shed some tears when he hugged me
He told me try not to worry I'd soon be free

It's easy for him to say, but it's hard in here
He assured me he loved me dear
Before you knew it the time was gone
He said he would visit again, it won't be long

Time was up, my visit was at an end
I told my dad I was going round the bend
I told my dad I was very upset
When I tried to take my life, I didn't have no regrets

He said he'd promise he would write
Was there something I would like?
I told him please don't make promises,
He would probably not keep
But I told him I'd probably wouldn't lose any sleep

Our Dad

CP

Two hands together working to pleasure our faces,
Beautiful blooms neatly arranged full of colour,
Fence given an extra coat to outstand other gardens,
As summer approaches, the smell of cut grass aromas the air,
Bringing tears to sore eyes,
From neglect to death, the garden
Has been given a new lease of life,
Tendered by those hardworking hands,
No job, no money, but an impressive gathering
Of healthy growth in the garden,
Especially cultivated for beauty and pride,
Patience is a virtue and rewarding,
A place to relax and breathe with happiness,
Those hands, those aged, cracked embracing hands,
Will start again tomorrow,
Weather permitting.

America

NR

America
Big living
Unknown grounds
Opportunity giving
Unreal but realistic
Unviolated love
Sunny August mist
Lighting bugs in simple flight
Corn crops growing over the top
Dreamland for a while
Rules never broken
Kind heart been given
Everlasting memory in my heart
America

Waiting(2)

JJ

The green beneath my feet
Swirls in a still movement
Rhythms and hypnotic
Uniformity discretely hidden
Soft yellow surrounds me
Glistening sunlight captured
Encased in this moment
In this place

Jasmine drifts in the air
Lightly uplifting
Contrasted with the weight
Of roses on the breeze
I sit on my wooden seat
The bare brick wall behind me
Surrounding this enclosure
The garden of a waiting room

Far From Home

V

I was born in Panevezys in Lithuania. I was born in prison hospital. I stayed with her in prison till she was released. When she was released I was adopted by my grandmother, Alfonca. I lived with her all my life until I was eighteen and came to England.

I lived in a small village called Pumpienai. About five hundred people lived there. There were two or thre shops that sold food cleaning stuffs for the home.

When I lived with my Grandma (babute) in a long house where there were two flats one after the other. I would have eggs and bread for breakfast with coffee or tea. About eight o clock I leave the house and go to school. About twenty minutes to school. I liked school because I could make friends, My cousin Mantas was in the same class. We spend our time together because we live in the same village. When I come home from school I go to his house to play.

Later on I was naughty at school. I didn't listen. I ran away from the class. When I was fifteen, before on Christmas me and my friends get drunk and there is a fight and I was expelled and went to another school. To do this I had to go back and live with my Mum. I don't like living there because my mum was always drinking and she lived too far from my grandmother.

So I escaped from where my mum lived and went off with my friends. This was to show my family that I did not want to live with my mum.

Louise's Story

Taking care of someone else

S

She was three years old. She was happy. She thought that the love surrounding her would never change. But soon she learned that her whole life was about to be ripped away from her in one swift move

Her parents split and Louise went with her mum. She was scared. She felt alone. As the years went by her trust in everyone slowly began to mend. By the time Louise was six years old her auntie was getting her to look after her two kids – one aged four was a lovely little girl and the other was a baby boy, a week old who just wanted to be held.

Louise was just a child herself. She didn't understand a thing about looking after two children, especially ones with no Dad. Her brother Ben was out having fun. Her mother was out all night and slept all day. Her Auntie Jane was the only adult around and then that wasn't often. While Jane was out shopping Louise was looking after Jane's kids.

By the time Louise was eight years old her mum had left her and her brother Ben. Ben took care of Louise for two weeks but they soon ran out of food and clean clothes so Louise ended up living with Andrea and Ben with their grandparents.

Louise thought her life might get better but she was sorely mistaken. Her life was going to get worse and worse in the next year.

Louise's Auntie Jane beat her every day and life was going from bad to worse. Louise had to look after her cousins Kayliegh and John . With them being so young and defenceless Louise had to make sure that they didn't get beaten.

Soon things got even more difficult because Louise was spending more and more time in hospital because of Jane beating her.

After just over a year Louise had had enough. It took her just over a month to find her brother Ben and her mother. Then one day when Auntie Jane was out Louise packed her things and got the kids and left the house. She got on a bus and travelled from one end of the city to the other. It took just over an hour for Louise to reach her mother's house.

Louise was scared that her mother might not want to know her. But she just put away her fears and went to the door and walked in. She shouted, 'Mum, Mum! Please, please let me come home and let Kayliegh and John stay. I don't want to go back there again.'

She sat down and told her mother everything. Her mother could only say, 'I'm sorry Louise. You can come. But I can't have Kayliegh and John as they are not my kids.'

So the next day Louise's Mum took Kayliegh and John home. Louise was upset for a long time after that but she tried to see the kids every day to make sure they weren't taking the beating for her leaving.

By the time Louise was eleven years old her Mum had gone through about twelve different men but soon settled down with a nice man. But Louise was determined not to give him a chance and this ended up badly.

By the time Louise was twenty years old she was in jail, married and her mother moved away. Louise's brother Ben tried his best to be there for his little sister but things weren't as easy as they sound.

By the time Louise was twenty five years old she had written her own novel and got her own house and had three businesses. She was married, surrounded by friends, but most of all she was surrounded by love for the first time. Now Louise was truly happy, just like she had been when she was three years old before her father left.

SHH!

NR

Shsh .. be as quiet as a mouse
Cause there are secrets in this house
Shsh ...don't make any noise please
Cause there are secrets in my house
Shsh ... be as quiet as a mouse
Cause there are secrets in my house
Like Mum bumped her face on the table
And I keep falling downstairs
Shsh ... be as quiet as a mouse
Cause there are secrets in my house
Shsh .. be as quiet as a mouse
Cause there are secrets in this house
Please! as I beg and plead
Not to tell daddy
Shsh ... be as quiet as a mouse
Cause there are secrets in my house

Early Morning Blue

Just like now, caught in the revolving door, in and out, swearing never to come back…

Novel Extract 2

AMJ

Chapter 2

It's sausages for tea. And wrinkled spuds, spooned-up beans and a rinsed out salad Even though I don't like the look of the sausages, even though they remind me of a butcher's fingers on a winter's day, I hold out my plate. I need hot food because despite the heat I had woken from tea-time bang-up feeling cold. I look around the dining hall, it's already half full of women and more than full of noise. I make my way to the far corner and sit down with Mandy and Angela, next to the window. I'm right about the sausages; they're dangerous. Raw and pink…

'Bernadette, Bernadette.'

'Yes.'

'What the fuck do you call this woman?'

'I don't know.'

'I said what the fuck do you call this? Call this a fucking dinner?' He picks up a piece of sausage and squashes it between his thumb and first finger, hard, then holds it up to her face, 'You're a fucking disgrace you are. That's what you are you whoring bitch.'

FIST

'Can I have your sausages, if you don't want them T?' asks Mandy. I push them over to her plate.

'You're looking good,' I say to Angela, who has blow dried her hair and put her make-up on, 'isn't she Mandy?'

'Yeah, she is. You had a visit?'

'I wish,' said Angela, 'no, you fannies, it's library tonight, init. He'll be in tonight.'

'Ooh, who? Mr Paul?'

'That's right.'

'He's got B.O. Don't like 'm,' says Mandy through mouthfuls of chewed up sausage.

'Never said I liked him, girls, now did I? It's not about like, now, is it?'

'Needs must,' I say. It was something I got from my mother.

'Exactly,' says Angela putting down her knife and fork and raking her fingers through her peroxide blonde, 'if I want my perfume and my CDs and my bit of make up then I've got no choice. Besides he hasn't got B.O. –that's you.'

She directs this at Mandy who doesn't seem to notice and asks, 'What's for pudding?'

'I haven't got time for pudding. He'll be here by now and there's barely an hour before bang up,' says Angela getting up from the table and taking her plate to the hatch.

'Come on we'll go and see what they've got,' I say to Mandy and we join the pudding queue –women idling, gathering, lolling, every kind of woman, who wants pudding that is, and that is most women, because let's face it in this place pudding can be a serious, hard core, light you up comfort trip, though to be truthful it's just as likely to be a scabby horse of disappointment. Mandy's happy with jam roly-poly, I go for the rice pudding - bad choice. When Mandy has seen off the roly-poly and custard and my rice pudding we head for the library.

It's small, the library, and when the association room's closed it gets packed with women who don't really want to be there. It's like the swimming baths when the kids are off. It upsets me to see it like that. Sometimes a fight starts up and someone has to push the panic bell and the screws come running and the library gets closed down. I suppose you could say it's everything a library shouldn't be, except sometimes, when they're all in association and there's just a few in, the few who really want to get a book out, or sometimes in the day, when Peter brings us over from the gardens and lets us spend an hour there. I'm happy then.

It was the books that kept me going, before I met Landy and started running away, before she died. All kinds of books, every kind of book including the ones we wrote in at school, feint- lined with margins, squared paper for graphs, better for words, letters fit just right in the squares. Books kept things right and I kept them tidy, those exercise books, just as neat and tidy as I could. I hated it if I got a dog- eared corner or a blot of ink from a leaky biro or if I made a crossing out. If I did, that was it, because once a page was spoiled it had to come out. Everyone else in the class thought I was weirdo, mad, but I had to keep the whole thing right and besides I was always praised for my neatness and my handwriting, so fuck them.

I wasn't much interested in the books we had at home, they were my father's war stories. When he was sober he did a fair bit of reading but always as far as I could see about soldiers and war. My mother read mainly gardening magazines. When my father was reading things were cool. You could relax. It was when he closed a book in that deliberate way of his, clapping the covers together with hands like paddles, when he stood up and put the book back on the shelf, looked at his watch and fetched his jacket, that was when you moved it and if you had any sense you got ready for bed. That was when my mother fussed about making sure everything was in its place and his supper left between two plates for when he got back from the pub. That was when you best be on your guard, when the first ripple of fear turned in your stomach and you prayed that if you were good enough and everything was truly in its place, that he would collapse on the couch and lie, mouth open, grunting and snoring like a buffalo. How you prayed. I'm not ashamed to admit I prayed and prayed especially to St Theresa:

St Therese, the Little Flower, please pick me a rose from the
Heavenly garden and send it to me with a message of love

I learned that much at school, after that it became mine..

And while you're about it St Therese please pick a rose for Bernadette, my mother

And please make sure that my father doesn't come home drunk again

And get mad and go beating her up. Please…

Amen

I stopped praying when the snoring started.

But to get back to the books. They melted the fear. It might be winter in the house, with the wind howling and storms raging but inside the pages of my book it was high summer and I was Eustacia Vye roaming wild on Egdon Heath.

It was a shame my teachers said, that I didn't stick in more, didn't always turn up. Tommo even came to the house one summer and drank tea with my mother in the garden, took his jacket off in the heat and asked if there was anything wrong. My mother did her best to disguise the bruises on her face and arms. I think by that time he'd stopped beating me.

By then it was too late. I'd already started nicking stuff you see. Little things at first and the odd book, not designer gear like now and not for the drugs. My apprenticeship I suppose you could call it. Sometimes things I didn't even want or books I could have got from the library. I think it was just the bad blood in me. And in the beginning it was fun and I wrote everything I got down in a waxy covered red notebook but soon there was too much to keep under my bed and before long I was caught in it, in a trap of steal and get rid and steal again, as if I had no choice. Just like now, caught in the revolving door, in and out, swearing never to come back but heading out and straight for trouble. Some people are made like that and I'm one of them. Ask Landy, he knows, he's seen the worst of me, he knows what I'm capable of.

A Lovely Thought

SS

What a lovely thought, I got a card
Shirley made it, she said it wasn't hard
It said sorry for my loss, some girls signed it
It was appreciated, it made me think and sit

It can be hard when you lose someone
So it was nice what Shirley had done
I was feeling sorry for myself and thinking it's not fair
But I was amazed by how many girls did care

So thank you for your appreciation it was kind
I didn't expect anything, I'm glad you had me in mind
My aunt's at peace now and gone to a better place
She's not lost the battle, but she's won the race

School Uniform

Amelia was very awkward when it came to choosing shoes
NR

One afternoon when Amelia was eleven years old Mark drove Amelia, Josephine and Gemma to Wigan town centre because they needed to get their school uniforms as this year Amelia was going to high School. On the way there Mark told Gemma to be on her best behaviour and to make sure to tell him if Amelia does anything wrong. Amelia piped up and said, 'Why do I always do wrong even before I have done it?'

Mark told her to, 'Shut up or you'll stay in the car with me' Amelia soon became quiet and Gemma agreed to do as Mark said.

Amelia was angry at her sister and her mum for not sticking up for her. They got out the car and walked to Ethel Austin's to buy socks and underwear, Amelia choose ankle socks and socks that go to your knees. Gemma didn't like Amelia's choice in socks and she choose multi coloured ones.

Josephine told Gemma and Amelia not to choose shoes over £15 because she couldn't afford them as Mark only gave her enough money to buy what they needed. And so they could go to MacDonald's if they had enough money left over.

Amelia was very awkward when it came to choosing shoes as she went through them like no tomorrow. All the shoes she liked Josephine said were no good or too expensive so only Gemma got shoes. They were black shiny boots which went to the ankle. Amelia liked them but they didn't do them in her size. Josephine got very pied off with Amelia over the shoe situation and decided to go to Slater's for the rest of their uniforms.

After that they had enough money to go to MacDonald's, Josephine asked her daughters not to tell their dad that they went to MacDonald's. 'You see Mark hates MacDonald's and doesn't think it is worth the money.' But for Josephine it was one of her favourite foods and she loved treating her kids to it from time to time.

Amelia stated she wanted to find some shoes before they go but Josephine said they couldn't afford to now until next week. Amelia started to throw a fit and started to cry but Josephine tried to explain but it was no good, so they left MacDonald's and started walking to the multi-storey car park where Mark said he'd be waiting for them. Josephine asked Amelia to please stop crying before we get up to the car park top. She stopped crying and Josephine wiped her face and Amelia asked her mum not to tell her dad but Gemma butted in and said, 'If mum doesn't tell I will!'

Amelia started yelling at her mum to make Gemma stop and not tell their dad.

Josephine said, 'She isn't going to say anything,'

Gemma butted in again and said, 'I am telling, dad told me to'

Amelia started to panic as they reached the top of the multi-storey car park and Mark was sat there in his white Mondeo eating two cheese pies.

Mark saw them coming and Gemma started running towards the car. As she got there Mark got out and asked how it went. Gemma looked back at Amelia and her mum and told her dad that Amelia took a fit because she didn't get any shoes. Mark got hold of Amelia by the arm and asked Josephine why she didn't get any shoes. Josephine tried to explain and stick up for her daughter but Mark wasn't having any of it.

He told Josephine and Gemma to get into the car. Josephine did as he said and Mark asked Amelia, 'Why can't you just behave?'

She answered and said, 'Sorry' but Mark wouldn't listen. He just dragged Amelia to the edge of the multi-storey car park and asked Amelia to look over the edge. As she did Mark grabbed her legs and hung her over the car park wall.

Amelia was screaming and crying in fear. He was going to let her go and throw her over the wall. Josephine dashed out the car and ran to Mark where she started yelling at him to bring Amelia back over the wall.

As he did this Amelia was shaking and crying and Mark said, 'That is the last time you defy me. Now get into the car before I slap you silly.'

Amelia got into the car and they drove home in silence when they got back Amelia went straight to her room for doing wrong.

Heaven

NR

I felt so very sad because
My stupid Dad ate all my tomorrows
Clouds felt close and it made me think
I'd been so bad. But I can't have been bad
Because I'm going to Heaven, leaving
My world behind, In heaven I'll find
All my true friends, happiness without end

I'd Fly To You

JA

I lie here
I whisper your name
Like it's only a game
Then I think of
The times we had
And I want to fly to you
Open the door
And spread my wings
And fly to you

You're an only child
But in your eyes
I see your pain
It's me to blame
I want to
Take you in my arms
Hold you once again,
Then call out your name
I want to fly to you

So, open the door
Let me be free
So I can fly to you
Take you from your pain
Dance and sing again
My little one
In the sunshine
And the rain.
I want to fly to you

David's Quest

L

Novel extract:

Spoiled, self absorbed David becomes obsessed by his mother's friend Miriam and when she falls into a coma, goes to the far side of the world to find a cure for her.

...David pushed a gold handle down and the heavy ebony door swung open, Miriam followed him., Although she herself was a successful wealthy woman, the magnificence of the house never ceased to amaze her, Eva seemed to have a wonderful flair for interior design, this house seemed gothic yet with a touch of the orient about it, probably due to the colour scheme: red carpet complemented the thick sheepskin rugs, a crystal chandelier which would have looked tacky anywhere else hung in the hall, and lent itself perfectly to the understated yet poignant black wrought iron candlestick holders, with large red scented candles on either side of the hall.

Miriam had a fleeting memory of an expedition she had undertaken as a student, examining the behaviour of the killer bee and its venom in Africa. She wondered if these candles were beeswax.

'Mother, there's someone here to see you' David hollered

His elegant mother appeared in a sleeveless royal blue ankle length Versace dress, her flaxen hair pulled tightly into a bun with a few strands loosely falling around her face. She wore a haughty yet excited expression and her tall slim frame seemed to shudder when she saw Miriam, 'Darling, how wonderful to see you, I've been out of sorts lately,'

Miriam dodged the air kisses subtly as Eva greeted her. 'Come in! Do tell me what's been going on, I'm afraid I've been drinking more than my usual two glasses of red,

David snorted at this comment and sneered under his breath, 'Two bottles more like'

Eva ignored him and continued to blame herself, privately berating herself for drinking before dinner time. She knew this was becoming a habit. 'Let's go sit in the drawing room'

Eva led Miriam into a familiar place where she sat and marvelled at the bearskin hung on the wall and the beautiful oil paintings that adorned the place. Miriam always felt at home here, her friend and host was always so welcoming and charming, Even if she was drunk a lot of the time, the elegance she possessed didn't seem to wane.

Eva ushered Miriam into a black leather chesterfield, then went to the drinks cabinet and poured her a large scotch that would have been a treble measure in any bar,

'Steady on Eva,' said her son.

'Oh don't be such a bore, David darling. What are you having?'

'Nothing at this time of day, I'm not joining alcoholics anonymous by the time I'm 30 because of you'

'A simple no thank you would have sufficed,' his mother said, wondering where on earth he got his character from,

'Where's John?' Miriam asked

'Oh he'll be back in ten. He's popped to the wine-shop because we're running low on red wine.' She laughed heartily at this, as though it were hilarious,

'He's probably gone to drive his car off the end of a cliff somewhere to get out of spending the rest of his vacation with you,' said David.

'Oh David please shut up, you really are becoming so tedious.' said Eva.

Miriam stared intently at David, willing him to shut up, which he did, for a while.

Eva held her glass in the air after handing Miriam her scotch and declared a toast.

'A toast to all of us,' Then her blue eyes flashed confusion and she quickly shook her head and downed her own large glass of whisky and soda in one. Eva sat down and surveyed the room through glazed yes,

'Well Eva, I'm going to dash I know it's been a flying visit but I feel rather faint,' declared Miriam.

David responded to her straight away, 'God, are you ok? You look as white as a sheet, Mother what have you done, giving her a measure like that? You know she doesn't drink,'

'Oh it's not Eva's fault David,' said Miriam. 'I've felt out of sort for a few days,'

Eva attempted to stand up and slumped back into her chair listlessly,

'Oh for God's sake woman' said David 'Go back to sleep'.

The hurt was obvious on Eva's face even in her intoxicated state.

'Sit down a minute,' he said to Miriam. 'I'll get a doctor,'

'No David, really I'll be fine, it's probably nothing'.

Eva half listened to what was being said and wondered at her son's concern for Miriam. Why he couldn't extend the same level of empathy to her? A twinge of jealously sobered her up a little, and she sat upright now, her hair tousled and an expression of irritation on her face, 'David get a doctor! She's not OK at all,'

'But she doesn't want one, Mother,' he replied. Then he went into the kitchen and made Miriam an espresso, courtesy of his mother's top of the range coffee machine. After relaxing for a while and making small talk with a increasingly sober Eva, Miriam seemed ready to leave. 'Oh darling I'm so sorry.'

'God don't be stupid,' said Eva, you can't help being ill'. Then stupidly she added 'It must be the hot flushes'.

Miriam thought if only she was starting to go through the menopause now.

But that was many years ago, 'Really darling,' she said. 'I'll be fine'.

David called her a cab and seemed to be the personification of concern. Watching them together Eva tried to make the worm of envy stop wriggling about in the pit of her stomach before it turned into a boa constrictor.

As David put Miriam's bicycle into the boot of the cab he felt sorry that she had to leave so soon. He urged her to make an appointment with the doctor as soon as she arrived home. Even with her vast knowledge on an array of subjects she was uselely inadequate at looking after her own health, even though she exercised frequently, didn't smoke and rarely drank, She would have to be nearly at death's door before she went to the doctors , both she and David knew this. But David knew her well enough to know that if he phoned on her behalf that those would be seen by her as intrusive.

He stood at the kerb as the cab pulled away, an unfamiliar feeling, warm and pining, filled his cold heart, and he swore to himself that he was going soft. As he went back into the house he noticed that his mother was gently snoring in the drawing room and thought to himself, 'The useless cow'

He wondered why his dad had been so long because he fancied a game of chess.

In her apartment Miriam sat on her ancient two-seater with the multi-coloured hessian throw on it, talking to her friend Quentin on the cordless phone, about the only thing that was modern in the apartment. All her possessions had an other-worldly quality about them. Like Miriam herself, everything had an interesting origin about it. The throw she was sitting on originated from south east Asia when she was an expedition in her late twenties. She'd bought it from a local market in a small village she was staying at. The Indians, renowned for their use of bright colours and excellent quality dyes, had excelled themselves, even by their own standards, with this throw. Even after all these years the colours remained bright: the aquamarine blue, fused with the scarlet red and yellow ochre, in intricate geometric shapes.

Miriam fiddled with her parachute silk shawl as she chatted away to Quentin, explaining about how the horses would need to be transported. Nearing the end of the conversation she mentioned the cost in a roundabout way, Quentin wouldn't hear of her paying anything. When she insisted he replied in his quaint English way 'If you insist on paying then I won't help you at all.'

'Well that's that then,' replied Miriam'

Embarrassed yet grateful for her old friend's generosity and decency, she replaced the cordless phone on the coffee table, if such a mundane description could be used referring to this object where in place of legs was a granite elephant with its trunk upturned on which rested a semi-opaque circular surface of obscure glass.

She glanced at the elephant. At once wonderful memories of Asia flooded her mind, of all the beautiful continents she had visited, Asia, with its diverse culture and breathtaking scenery had impressed her senses the most. Even in the poverty-stricken suburbs she had found human kindness so stirring she almost felt ashamed to be British. Lost in her daydream and content with knowledge that the matter of David's mother had been taken care of, she allowed herself to fall into a deep sleep. Never one for resting during the day, this in itself was unusual for Miriam.

Back at Eva's house, David's father had returned, and placed the bottles of Merlot almost awkwardly on the kitchen table. David sitting there with his hands clasped behind his head explained to him how the woodland needed to be replaced completely. John sighed, 'Well its not my fault.'

It obviously was because if he had listened to his father about the matter of the Scandinavian pine in the first place then none of this would have happened.

John listened to David first ranting on about the pine, and then Chimera's[3] illness, then finally about his mother and how she was 'pissed again'. He stood there with his back to David, spreading butter on a slice of toast on the marble worktop, and felt consumed by an unfamiliar emotion, rage. It brewed up inside him like a poison, He spun around and shouted, 'You selfish bastard, shut your fucking ungrateful mouth!'

David looked shocked and bewildered, He had never heard his father swear, let alone raise his voice to this ear splitting volume 'Dad don't shout at me!'

'SHUT UP NOW AND GET OUT OF THIS KITCHEN, LEAVE ME ALONE!'

David left the kitchen, but not before glancing over his shoulder to see his mild-mannered, kind Dad standing grimacing with rage, full of hate as he stared at David. The glasses that normally emphasized his gentleness, now served as magnifying glasses, reflecting anger and rage at his son for the first time in his life. Now David felt afraid of his own father, but as usual he was unable to understand that other people might have problems. Today he put it down to his father's over-working, neglecting to see that at present he was on holiday anyway.

David decided to go for a walk until things cooled off a bit. His mother's crystal tones echoed in his ears as he slammed the front door, 'Lunatics' he muttered to himself, 'David what's wrong with John?' was the phrase resounding as he left the house. His mother sounded genuinely upset, not that he registered it as her walked aimlessly around the neighbourhood.

[3] *NB his horse…*

Back home John sat with Eva, his arms wrapped around her as she cried. He felt sad himself but wanted to remain strong for his wife. He saw outward displays of emotion as a weakness and didn't want to lose control twice in one day by crying. He wondered if he had been harsh with David or whether the boy had deserved it, but he knew that the way he had dealt with David was probably called for.

David cursed at himself quietly under his breath, wondering what was the point of circling the neighbourhood like this, 'I'll go and see Miriam', he half thought aloud, 'I'm worried about her anyway.' He strode purposefully towards the nearby village. It was only four miles he thought, The prospect of going home to collect his bike didn't seem like a good idea at present.

He walked past a group of teenage girls standing in a bus stop and they started whistling at him. Without looking twice at them he muttered, 'Sluts', and continued walking in his angry determined way. He thought he'd take the short cut through the park. That would cut at least a mile out. As he strode through the park he kicked at the gold and russet leaves which lay like nature's confetti on the warm autumn ground. He broke into a jog, then a sprint, and must have looked an impressive sight to any onlooker, his powerful legs pounding the earth, with leaves becoming displaced and his dark hair blowing in the autumn breeze like strands of black fire.

As the adrenaline started pumping, David thought about how he had never broken into a purposeful sprint in his life, yet here he was running to Miriam as though his life depended on it. He slowed his pace as he neared the six foot fence that led onto the estate where Miriam lived. He cleared it effortlessly, just as a horse might clear a jump. His feet barely seemed to make contact with the ground as he levered his lithe frame over the top of the fence and landed expertly onto his feet.

He paused for a moment to smooth back his hair and walked calmly onto the small road then onto the footpath at the left. He could see Miriam's apartment from here. The whole place reminded him of a retirement village. He remembered his parents looking about here when they wanted to downgrade from the previous over-the-top sprawling Georgian Mansion that they had lived in a few years ago. David remembered vividly the fuss he had made when his dad suggested living in a quiet area full of thatched cottages and semi-modernized apartments 'I'm not living in granny houses,' he had said.

As he approached the elegant apartment with its whitewashed walls and climbing ivy he took a deep breath of the autumn air and pressed the intercom button that was named 'Miriam Swan' in shiny black italics on a white background. After quite a time had passed, an impatient David shouted, 'Miriam!'

On the off chance that her window was open, he turned around to see net curtains twitching in the neighbouring street 'nosey bastards' he thought. He shouted even louder this time 'MIRIAAAM!'

A small elderly man with an irritated look pushed the reinforced glass panel door and asked in clipped English tones, 'What's all the noise about, boy?'

David snarled in response 'I'm worried about my friend Miriam, let me in'.

The man stood hesitantly and started to say 'You could be anyone.'

David seized the opportunity. He grabbed hold of the man's wrist whilst blocking the door with his foot, roughly shoved him out of the way and slammed the door behind him, The old man stood confused and dazed. 'Pull yourself together old boy,' snapped David' He emphasized the word boy, as the man had called him a boy, and he took offence at that.

He ran up the first two flights of stairs, pausing at Miriam's door. He banged loudly three times, then realised it was off the latch and entered, Sometimes I can be so stupid he thought to himself. He strode along the short passage and gasped as he caught sight of Miriam in the living room, her head tilted to one side. She was breathing in short metallic rasps,

'Oh my god,' he gasped. Knowing not to move her he went over to the phone and dialled 999. 'Ambulance!' he roared down the phone. After giving the address and explaining that Miriam was blue, he sat down and looked at her, willing the ambulance to be quick. He wanted to hold Miriam, to tell her everything would be OK. Hot tears stung at his eyes and he forced them back. He didn't want to cry at a time like this. For the first time he realized that his feelings for Miriam ran deeper than that old cliché 'just good friends.' 'Where's this damn ambulance?' he muttered, and then he heard a knock and a shout at the door.

'In here!' David screamed. The paramedics came in. The two large men almost David's size, but much broader, hoisted Miriam gently onto a stretcher and covered her with an orange insulation blanket. David explained in childish tones 'I didn't know what was wrong....I had just come in she was blue and breathing funny....She wasn't well earlier... had a drink at my mother's,' His disjointed sentences only added to the effect that he was slowly losing control, 'I want to go with her.'

'You can't,' came the curt reply, 'Stay here, lock up the apartment and contact the hospital in about an hour. Try to relax'. A patronising reply.

As the ambulance pulled away David realized that he had never felt as low in his life. He wandered, deflated, back into the apartment. The old man who David snapped at earlier stood in the stairwell. His face now epitomized concern, 'You know, she keeps taking turns, dizzy spells? I had to help her up the stairs last week, She refused to use the lift.'

'Ok, I'm sorry about earlier. I'm Eva's son, her friend Eva's son David'

'Oh yes I do remember her talking about Eva Sometimes I go in to have coffee with Miriam, you know.'

'Oh do you now?' said David almost angrily. He started climbing the stairs ignoring the old man muttering. 'Goes in for coffee does he?'

He went into the apartment, went to the airing cupboard and turned the central heating off. She must have been cold because it was boiling in here, she didn't strike him as someone who would feel the cold much.

The study was directly opposite the living room. Dusty books lined the myriad ebony shelves; bizarre- looking book stops not unlike gargoyles reared their ugly little heads here and there, their ugliness only serving to complement their morbid appeal.

David whiled away the hour looking at big boring manuals on microbiology, botany and medical books which read like relics to his modern mind. Then he said suddenly 'Hospital!' and phoned the hospital. He already had the number in his memory bank. He had been told once that he was in possession of a photographic memory, and that had only increased his arrogance. At least now he was using it for a good purpose.

After a brief conversation he didn't find out much, only that

Miriam was stable but still asleep. His mother Eva was down as her next of kin so it looked as though he was going to have to get her to the hospital to try determine exactly what was wrong with Miriam. They weren't likely to tell him;

Absentmindedly David picked up a brown folder from Miriam's desk and started leafing through the contents. Although he was still worried about Miriam he lost himself in the intricate detail of a catalogue of weird descriptions of plants. Latin names sat alongside carefully inscribed handwritten italics. The plants and fauna all had medicinal qualities or narcotic ones, which surprised David. He had never thought of Miriam being interested in drugs. The detail was incredible. There was even an in-depth description of a carnivorous plant that belonged to the Venus flytrap family, a cactus. Alongside it was a crudely drawn diagram of how the plant was capable of digesting a person from the inside out as their flesh disintegrated into a type of organic mulch.

It occurred to David that this folder was some type of research for a fictional novel, but as he leafed further through it a photograph dropped onto the desk. He picked it up as if it was going to bite him. There she was, a younger Miriam, standing in a long white kaftan with a wide brimmed straw sun hat on with what appeared to be the man eating plant. To her left, the foliage in the background suggested a tropical location.

David turned the photograph over and written on the reverse read in faded blue ink 'Discovery' found by Miriam Swan July 1960, Africa, then in brackets, almost comically 'somewhere in the jungle'

.

So, Miriam had discovered a rare species of plant, thought David in admiration. As he placed the photograph back inside the folder he read a few more pages in her handwriting of how this plant named 'Discovery' also had the power to restore coma victims as well as eating them. How the leaves could be infused to make an anti-aging serum. There were a whole host of other benefits including how the resin in the roots could cure malaria.

Miriam! David threw down the file and said out loud. 'Shit, how is she? How is she?'

He phoned his mother and explained how Miriam had been taken to hospital, then practically ordered her to go to see how Miriam was. Eva didn't need telling twice. David spoke to his Dad on the phone, telling him he'd wait in the apartment rather than return home. He had left in his childish rage and he had forgotten his house key.

Thirty minutes later the phone rang. David engrossed again in the folder, let it ring twice and then snatched it off the desk.

'She's in a coma.' A tearfu-sounding Eva seemed to pour down the phone and fill the vacant cavity which was David's anticipation 'Oh my god. ARE YOU SURE?'

He contemplated the coincidence of him reading about comas and cures and carnivorous plants and Miriam falling into a coma. He expected to wake up any moment, and this whole drama to come to an abrupt end.

But it did not.

Christmas Time's Supposed To Be Good

JA

Christmas time's supposed to be good
So what happened to my childhood?
Where are those years?
Where have they gone?

When I was young I loved you
But now I don't believe
Why did you take those dreams
Away from me?

Santa Claus you're just a miff
A figment, just a wish
But Oh My God suppose it's true
And I just imagined you

The Option Of Freedom

A woman becomes a writer on leaving prison

Short Story

WR

Two years after her release from prison, in her best selling book Behind the Door, poet Paulie Smith was to write:

The truth about what each woman had done, the truth about the life that led her to this place would come out in spurts and trickles among them. If it trickles out that a woman had anything to do with hurting children she suffered terrible sanctions which did not always harm the flesh but which sometimes seared the soul. A modified degree of truth would occasionally emerge. How a woman's co-accused had got off on bail while she was in here; how there was no proof; how the police concocted the proof; how a girl had been rugby-tackled by a store detective and banged from unit to unit by him and his colleague, how telephone numbers were taken and this meant that girl would get off despite actually putting the sliver figurine under her coat.

The people who knew most, if not all, of the story were the people who had the files, the people whose legitimate living was made out of the misery of these women: the professionals. Lawyers and psychiatrists, probation and prison officials; social workers. With these people the women were forced to be to be the most open, the most guileful, the most persuasive, the most poignant. With these people a woman had to present, or invent, a self that was worth saving, even worth liking, to take herself beyond the level of merely being a case. In some quarters this was labelled manipulative.

One thing for sure. You were part of the romance of their lives.

The man got up and came forward to shake Paulie's hand. 'Pauline Smith is it? I'm John Landsman. Miss Cornell would tell you I was coming to talk to you.'

'The brief?' She shook his hand, her hand soft in his. 'Sandy said you were a good psychiatrist,' she said. 'If you're as good a psychiatrist as she is a solicitor, then I'm in the fucken shit. She's missed three appointments out of four in the last month. Can't seem to get through the gate. She told me she hates all the rigmarole getting through the gate. I told her she must have a guilty conscience.' Paulie sat down and faced him across the table. 'If you're going to do word -association or show me inkblots like the last fucking shrink you can get lost,' she said.

'Now, Pauline,' he started. 'Miss Cornell does her best. She got me on board with your case.'

'My name is Paulie, if you want to use it. And I'll call you John.'

'Well, I don't think...'

'I tell you what. You don't call me Paulie, and I won't call you John.' She sat back in her seat.

'Do you want a cigarette?' he said, pushing an unopened packet towards her with a lighter on top.

She pushed it back. 'I don't smoke. You've been watching too many TV movies. And you've not read my file.'

He looked round, towards the door. 'Can I get you a cup of coffee?'

'I don't mind that.'

He came back to the bare little room balancing two cartons of coffee in his hand. He brought the smell of the prison in with him. 'I thought I'd join you, Paulie. Can we start again?' He smiled a faintly nervous smile, but his eyes were steady. He was younger than she'd first thought. His receding hair, cut short to his scalp, was deceptive. His face was young and open.

'I don't mind, John.'

They drank in silence for a few seconds. He tapped her weighty file, which was in front of him. 'Bit of a hard life, Paulie. But I have to admit, like you said, I didn't get round to every detail.'

'I wonder if your file's that thick,' she said examining him over the rim of her coffee cup. 'They'll have one on you, you know.'

'I want you to tell me about...'

'About what?'

'About your life. Anything.'

'Anything? Like the time I was high on magic mushrooms and went through the whole process of my own birth all over again?'

'Really?' He leaned back in his chair, his face bland, expressionless. 'I've heard this can happen.'

She drained the bitter coffee. 'Have you heard that in the middle of all that streaming light, that brilliant silver surging-forward, how someone heard their mother scream, heard their mother dying? Then their father sobbing?'

'No. No. I haven't heard that.' There was a long pause. He fiddled with his pencils. 'So your dad brought you up?'

'Well, I was fostered a short while, I think. After she died. When I was a baby. Then he brought me home and we clung together to survive the tide.'

He opened the file. 'I've read some of your depositions. I see you wrote them yourself. You have a way with words, Paulie.'

'Am I supposed to say thank you for that?'

'This is hard, Paulie. I have to be direct. We have so little time here. Can you tell me, in your own words, about your father?'

'My father was an angel. He worked and he worked with this great leaden weight on his back, the fact that he had lost her, my mother.' She kept her voice in neutral. 'I didn't know a night when he didn't cry. But he tried to be right with me. He really did. Read me stories. Taught me my numbers. Took me to the pictures. We saw 'Troy' together four times. Got me a book of Greek myths after that. Bought me a twelve volume encyclopoedia. When he was working, like. I could name every capital city in the world before I was seven. We had greasy take-aways and fish and chips and lots of eggs and beans. And potatoes. Just like prison food when you think about it.'

He made a note on his book. 'So the two of you, you coped all right?'

'Well, yes. Just about. Some people wouldn't approve of the way we were. He used to keep me up way past my bedtime and talk about the history of the world. The war. The Cold War. The nuclear threat when he was young. He was up on all that, thought everyone was about to get us. But always, even when I was very little, I still knew about this leaden weight on his back. Because of me she wasn't there. He'd lost her like he had lost a leg and an arm. He was crippled. Crippled for life. It was like he was shell-shocked, like those guys in the first world war. Did you see that film 'Regeneration'? All about that, that was. A neat film, that.'

'It was hard on a child, hard on you.'

She shrugged. 'It was hard on him. I understood that.'

'But it was hard on you,' he insisted. 'So small.'

She stared at him, then pushed her hand through her hair, spiking it up again. 'You don't understand.'

They sat for while in silence. She turned her plastic cup round and round on the stained table.

'So, you were coping?' He tried again.

'Him and me were all right. That was, till he was made redundant. The usual sob story. After thirty years etc. etc. Thought he was indispensable, he did.'

'And that was it?'

'That was it. That was when he started to drink seriously. Stopped going out. Sent me out for the booze and the cigarettes. A packet of groceries. He wouldn't go across the door. I've read about it since. Agoraphobia. We still talked quite a bit, him and me. He was still kind ... kind of ... interested in what I was up to. At school and that. Funnily enough I did all right at school.'

'Did no-one try to help?'

She laughed. 'Where have you been?No such thing as society, remember? He didn't want me to say about how he was. Not to tell anyone. He said they'd take me back into care. That he needed me. That it was me kept him alive.'

'The redundancy money wouldn't last forever, I suppose.'

'It didn't. He'd paid off the house. There was a little pension that paid the electric and gas. Then nothing.'

'What did you do then? What about unemployment benefit?'

'He wouldn't go out. Remember? Wouldn't go out of the house. You have to sign on. Didn't you know.'

'So what did you do?'

Paulie stood up and went to look out of the window. Two girls were trundling a dinner trolley along the path, shepherded by a prison officer who whistled as he walked along. 'Well, first I sold the encyclopoedias to a bookshop man ... anyway, you know what I did. It's in that file you've got there. You don't need to ask.'

'You tell me. I need you to tell me, Paulie.'

'I robbed the stuff we needed. Food. Clothes. Sold some, and we got along.'

'And you got him his booze?'

'Yeah. He couldn't manage without it.'

'But one day you got sick of all this.'

'That's right.'

'So you…'

'Ran away. Just for one night. I ran away to the coast. Spent the night in Woolworth's doorway. It was bloody freezing.'

'And when you got back…'

She turned round and leaned against the window. She was a black shadow against the bars. He couldn't see her face. 'And when I got back to the house he was dead, and if you want me to tell you about that you can go fuck yourself.'

'Yes. Right.' John Landesman shuffled the paper, flicked through the file, and made another note. 'You'd better come and sit down again, Paulie. If an officer comes in and finds you out of the seat he'll whip you away and our interview will finish.' He needed to see her face.

She sat down. 'I've read about it, since, you know. Spontaneous combustion. It comes somehow from inside of you. You burn slowly'.

He looked at her sharply. Her voice had lost its laconic drawl. It had a knife-sharp edge.

'I read about it, John. And I saw a programme on the TV. Since I was here inside.'

He shook his head. 'It's a myth, Paulie.'

'You're like the rest. All those do-gooders who talked on at me in that year after he died. Trying to make me say I'd done it. That I hated him and he had hurt me so I set the fire. But I didn't. So I wouldn't say, just to make them happy. They'd have been dead happy if I'd said that I did.'

'Then?'

'Then into care. Be the good girl. Into college. I was their pride and joy. Their success story.'

He flicked to a different part of the file. Then he took a cigarette himself, and lit it. It was a long time since he'd had a smoke. 'Tell me about Sebastian.'

She smiled faintly. 'My Sebastian had golden hair and a lot of charm,' she said. 'And he was a bad boy.'

'Bad …'

'Bad enough. He was a robber, a drug addict and a sponger.'

'Did he sponge on you?' John Landsman said the words too quickly.

She made him wait, then... 'It might have looked like that.'

'But you were teaching then … and he was a … a ne-er-do-well.'

She smiled openly. 'Now that's an old fashioned word, John Landsman. I wouldn't'a thought you were that old.'

His eyes narrowed. She noticed his long lashes as he lowered his gaze. 'I need to remind you, Paulie Smith, that your freedom's on the table here. Understanding what happened...'

'OK. OK ... Charlie was a ne-er-do-well. He robbed, he scrounged, he dug. But he had golden curls and a great charm.'

'Then you lost your job.'

'Well this feller Bernie, Sebastian's uncle, lost me my job. Poison pen letter. He was a wanker of the first order. Forgive me. Prison language. It seeps into you.'

He looked at her sharply, responding to her change of tone as though she had changed from a leopard to a lamb before his eyes. 'Why d'he do that? Sebastian's uncle?'

'Cause the old fart tried it on with me,' she said calmly. 'And I kneed him in the groin.'

'So he told the school authorities ...'

'That I was a nasty person. Unfit. Implied I was a junkie or worse. Then they got the knives out. No morals, growing up in care and that. All so sniffy that I walked out.'

John flicked his ash in the foil ashtray and waited.

'You should' a seen that letter, John. You won't find it in my file because – surprise, surprise - someone lost it! There he was, on the page baying for my blood. He said I swore I'd kill Sebastian because of another girl.'

'Is that true?'

She smiled. 'The only other girl in Sebastian's life was the White Prince.'

'Cocaine?'

'You've got it.'

'So. What did you do when you lost your job?'

'Well. Sebastian had this close shave with the cops, so he couldn't go out.'

'So?'

'I went out. Grafting. Shoplifting.'

He peered at the file. 'Very successfully, I believe.'

She shrugged. 'A living of sorts. It bought the food and the booze. It got him his fixes. And now you're looking for me to say this but actually it was like being back with my father,'

'Did you never use the stuff yourself?'

'If you look hard enough in the file you'll see I didn't . I did ... a few Es ... up till ... up till that happened to my Dad, but not since. Never since. It makes me vomit, anything like that. Never gets absorbed, so no hit.'

'Why do you think that is? '

She shrugged. 'I've read it somewhere. I'm not an addictive personality. Funny, that, isn't it? Not even booze. Sebastian was just the opposite, he was on everything. Except sex. So wrecked he couldn't manage that..'

John Landsman looked at her. 'Did you resent that? Why was that?'

'Resent?' She shook her head. 'My golden boy! Stoned half the time, couldn't rouse himself even when he was comparatively fresh. The drugs do that to them. But you know that, don't you?'

He looked at her carefully. 'You are very, very bright, d'you know that?'

'How kind of you!' She raised her brows, embarrassing him. Then she relented. 'I've always known it, but it's been bugger-all use to me so far. Just look at the file.' She looked at her watch. She suddenly felt very tired.

'Bear with me, Paulie. I know it's hard, but I just want you to tell me what you think happened to Sebastian.'

She sighed. 'Well, I've been out on the graft, I go to the pub where Sebby's usually waiting for me and the stuff. Six pairs of Donna Karan jeans. I'm pleased with myself, see? But Sebby isn't there. I give the jeans to the old bag that sells them on and I get back to the squat just in time to see the fire engines putting the fire out. Our stuff is in piles on the pavement. Sebastian's brass kettles. I look for my books ... all were burnt. D'you know I had two hundred and seventeen books? Spent all my spare on books.' She turned the plastic cup round and round on the formica top of the table. 'The old bag at the pub denies ever seeing me, so that puts me in the soup, time wise.'

'And Sebastian was burnt to … he died.'

'Yes. Sebastian died.' She pursed her lips.

'Can you tell me, Paulie, what you think happened?'

'It'll be in there,' she nodded at the bulky file. 'They say I set the squat alight, that I burnt Sebby. Don't they? And I say I didn't. I'm right about that, not them.'

'You tell me what you think happened?'

She took a very deep breath. 'I'd caught him at it before. He loved chips, did Sebby. Anything fried. He'd got me to get corn oil from the shop. Said he was gunna fry sausages. On the fire d'you see? We could only use the fire. No cooker. No power. But he liked frying on the fire. Said it was like being in the old Wild West. I told them about this other time I came back and Sebby'd been frying chips on the fire and had gone to sleep on the couch. When I came back the place was full of smoke. The fire had not caught in the room, though. Not that time. I came back in time to wake him up.'

'So you think this time it did? Catch fire?'

She nodded.

'And do you feel guilty, Paulie, about that? About ... leaving Sebastian to do that? To burn himself to death?'

She stared at him. 'Why should I feel guilty? I feel sad. I couldn't be more sad. He was a bad lad, but he had golden curls. I loved to wash his hair. Like I said, he had a great deal of charm.' She looked at her watch. 'Look, can I go? I've finished now. Nothing more to tell you.'

He closed the file and stood up. 'Thank you Paulie Smith. You've been very helpful.'

She was at the door. She turned to smile at him. 'Have I? But who have I been helping, John Landsman. You or me?'

He glared at her. 'The right report from me could get you out of here, do you know that?'

She stared at him and shrugged her shoulders.

It is dark but not pitch dark. Adrenaline is running through my brain like larks. I'm awake but not woken by a dream. It is some thing outside. Outside of me. The light is luminous pearl. I stretch my eyes wide; the magnet that is me pulls light through the crack between the salt-green curtains.

The dark dissolves into light, I can make this thing out now. Above me. Hanging above me. Hanging, not floating: a tangle of black rope or thick wool. It doesn't quite have the form of a spider's web but still it contains the same whispering menace.

I slip out of my body and swim across to the door, looking in vain for the handle. Of course. There wouldn't be a handle. No handles in here. I raise my hand to batter the panelled wood but make no more sound than if I were beating pizza dough or bubble wrap. I hold my hands up against the pulsing light and, peering closely, see that my fingers are bleeding and my nails are broken.

I slip back across into my body and now I watch that girl at the door, that girl who is Paulie Smith.I watch her and think what a pity it is. Those hands! Not mine. . My fingers are neat. Always neat. Filed oval with white tops, in the French style for that natural look. There is no reason to spoil them. Surely?

From: Behind the Door
Paulie .Smith

I ran around with your heart

JA

I ran around with your heart
I played the game
You played your part, like
An actor on a stage

I hear you call my name
Like a singer with a song
I often wonder
Where I went wrong

So take my heart
And let me apologise
Look in my eyes and
You will see what you mean to me.

The Other Side of Me

LJ

Hello, my name is Stevie. I am a thirty two year old woman, woman, yes woman. I have never introduced myself as a woman before, but recently I have discovered that I am a woman.

I come from a large industrial city in the North West of England. I was first of five children and was in fact born in a prison. However this is about me and not my family and I do not believe that being born in a prison had anything to do with who I became. In fact up until the age of twelve I was happy, my mum made sure that we always at the best food, dressed in expensive designer clothes and lived in a beautiful house. Me and the rest of my mum's kids always looked fantastic. We were the envy of all the other kids in our neighbourhood. I believe that my childhood was normal until I was twelve.

So, why now at the age of thirty two am I telling my story, why I am questioning who I am? One thing that I have not mentioned so far is that I am gay, I have always know that I am gay, I am happy with that and make no secret of my sexuality. I have never had a sexual relationship with a man, never fancied a man and am convinced that I never will. I do not hate men, in fact many of my friends are men and I love them as friends. I have never been sexually abused by a man and am gay by choice. So it has nothing to do with sexuality!

Well here I go! I am thirty two years old, female and gay. I am a shoplifter, currently in jail and I have been in and out of jail since I was fifteen years old. I have been in jail at least fifty times in seventeen years. I am a 'smack head', addicted to Heroin, Crack, and Valium and just about anything I can inject, swallow, snort or smoke. Just to put the icing on the cake I have been a 'smack head' since I was twelve years old!

Forget the gay bit, it is not a problem. Very recently I said to somebody, 'I want rid of this Stevie, this Stevie is a horrible bastard and I want to find the real Stevie!' It is very hard for me to admit but a few days before, I had cried, in fact sobbed for most the day and this somebody knocked on the door of my cell and asked if he could come in. I cannot remember if I answered or not be he came in anyway. He offered his hand as he always does; I squeezed it and said, 'I want my mum'.

I am a thirty two year old woman crying and sobbing like a twelve year old girl asking for her mum. For the first time in my life I said 'I am frightened', sorry it was the second time, the first being when I went for my first session of counselling with this person. I will call him Billy.

Very briefly I met him on the wing. He was a perfect target, stood on his own, obviously very new to prison. I bounced up and said, 'Who are you, lad?'. He said 'Billy, who are you?' I did not answer but said, 'What are you doing here?' He said 'I don't know. I must be mad, I used to have a good job and now I am stood here shitting myself!'

I laughed, and walked away and said, 'I am a smack head'.

I saw him a couple of times after that.

I discovered he was a Mental Health person, pointed to my head and said,'Can you sort this out?' And he said 'Only you can do that'.

Two days later I was sent to the block, seg, CSRU, call it what you wil, I was accused of bullying. Billy lad turns up to do the Meds, I was mithering for Methadone. 'Macbeth'. And he says 'Oh shit! Not you.'

A lot of things happened in the next few days. Billy offered to work with me. An officer informed me that she would be working with me. I have never been so pissed off in my life. I hated this officer and believed that she hated me. No way was she is getting the better of me! I told Billy, 'She can fuck off, I am not working with her.' He said,'Seems like you have not got a choice, best give it a try.'

I have hated this officer for over six years but now I trust hor and like her, what has happened to me! More so, I am beginning to like and understand more officers and governors.

I think the answer is that I have had enough. I have always accepted prison as part of my life but now I have had enough, not only of prison but of drugs and this bastard called Stevie. I want to change, but do not know how to do it.

So now we have a thirty two year old streetwise, smack-head trusting and making friends with screws and a nutcase called Billy! How weird is that!

I am supposed to be a hard nut, dressed in men's clothes,

covered in battle scars and tattoos, as hard as nails, couldn't give a fuck what anybody thought of me, gay and proud of it! Wherever I go, on the street or in prison people want a part of me, they want to be around me. If you have a problem go to Stevie, she will sort it. Somebody giving you a bad time Stevie will beat the shit out of them! All you need to do is give her a bit of smack in return. I never pay for drugs in prison, I sort out other people's problems and they thank me, usually with drugs!

I never believed I went looking for fights but, how much do I like a good fight, I love it! I get a massive buzz from it. Claret (blood), the more I see the more I want to see, I even become sexually aroused by it! People who hung around me would congratulate me. I believed I was untouchable, anyone who fancied their chances were welcome to have a go! I had an army of followers and admirers, nobody crossed me. In the prison and on the streets everybody loved Stevie. I was never short of a friend.

Being gay and in prison also has its advantages. Fifty times in prison and a new lover nearly every time, how good is that! I have had only two proper serious relationships and I got hurt. It hit me hard so I swore to myself I would never again get feelings for another girl. My motto was use and abuse because I thought that what all they were good for rag bag and bin bag.

Wherever I go my reputation has already got there. People hid from me, other people take a chance and try to make friends with me.

So a pretty scary person. Well there is more. Some years ago I saw a psychiatrist who told me that I have a personality disorder. Personality disorder or PD is basically a modern term for psychopath. Here we go thief, jailbird, smack head, aggressive psycho lesbian. Well, nobody in their right mind would want to meet one of these, in daylight let alone in a dark alley would they? Unfortunately many have and suffered.

Mention those two letters PD, Oh my god PD, nasty, horrible people, prisons full of them. They can't be trusted, they constantly tell lies, steal, bully, swear and fight. They really are a pain in the arse! You wouldn't take one home; in fact you wouldn't even tell one where you live. Well that's me. The only bit I do not agree with is 'bully'. That is until this officer who I used to hate but now like, explained to me what bully means.

I behaved the way I behaved because it is the only way I know.

If somebody does wrong they get battered, full stop, end of story. By taking notice of this officer it's about time she had a name so I will call her prison officer I now understand why other people see me as a bully.

If you are reading this, well I am sorry but this is the way it is or hopefully it was. I do not expect anybody to understand or forgive me. I would like a second chance and I would like to find me, but how can I ask people to trust me when I have never been able to trust myself? I have already acknowledged that I am a scary person. I am scared of me! I am scared of the old Stevie, he is not a nice person, he is an evil person but at the moment I still need to hide behind him, the armour and mask that he is until I am brave enough to be me!!

Confused? So am I. I introduced myself as Stevie a thirty two year old woman. Now I am referring to Stevie as a man but he is not really a man, he is somewhere between a boy and a teenager who got lost and became a thug! He has been stoned or at least semi-stoned for twenty years.

I can't believe I am saying this, in fact if you were telling me this story I would be saying bollocks, are you kidding me. To tell the truth I would probably say 'fuck off' and get up and walk out. What is even more unbelievable is that I am now referring to Stevie as he. Where the fuck did he come from?

I cannot undo what I have done, I could apologise, say sorry a million times but no one would believe me. I could ask you to feel sorry for me but I won't because it is not your fault and I would not expect you to show me any pity. Quite frankly I don't want any.

The more I say the more ashamed I become, but the more scared I become as well. I was transferred to the seg, the block for bullying, so what? I can do the block. I can do anything that these bastards throw at me. Well without drugs and my wing I started feeling insecure, even paranoid. On top of this I had this officer and a nutter called Billy(who has everybody standing around being a tree), pecking at my head!

So here goes, at least from those few weeks I learnt this. When I was twelve years old I had this job of seeing my younger brother and sister to and from school. I was proud of being in charge; I was caring for them and protecting them.

One day when we arrived home from school a tractor was parked across the road. My brother was full of energy, up to all sorts of mischief. Once he climbed onto a roof, fell through it and survived. I loved that little lad. I had sisters but he was my only brother. So this tractor, well, he bounced over to it. He wanted to climb onto it, he wanted a ride. I said, 'Go on then'. He jumped, the tractor started, the bucket swung round and in instant he was dead!

I am not making any excuses here, I am only trying to explain why I am the way I am. As I said before I cannot change the past or all the horrible things I have done. I am not looking for sympathy.

I picked him up, held him in my arms and was relieved because his eyes were wide open! How was I, a twelve-year-old girl supposed to know that those wide opened eyes meant that he was dead! By then my dad had arrived, his hair was literally stood on end. I then knew that my brother was dead. Well I went schizophrenic, I was hitting and kicking every man I could see demanding to know who the driver was.

I need to move on now. Where is that gay, hard nut, smack head, psycho gone just when really need him, her, it, whatever Stevie is?

Now Billy the nutter who thinks he is a tree is telling me that my current situation of who I am is linked to my brothers' death and unresolved grief. He is suggesting that I have a cupboard full of events in my life that I have not dealt with. He is telling me that this cupboard is full of little Stevies all jumping about wanting to be heard. He is telling me that the doors of this cupboard have burst open and no matter how hard I try I can not get the cupboard to close. How mad is that, he tells me that this cupboard is in my head? How the fuck can you get a cupboard in your head?

There is one person in my life that I fear, one person in my life who I love and one person who stands by me and gives me anything I want. All these three people are my mum.

For twenty years I believed that she blamed me for my brother's death. For twenty years I have believed I was to blame and in fact have taken the blame. More so I have now started blaming my mum for the way I am. I can't cook, wash my own clothes, look after myself, take responsibility. I ask she gives!

However Billy the tree explains that PDs do this. In fact having a diagnosis can give you an excuse. He also explains that if professionals are unable to explain why you behave the way you do they often say you are a PD. Problem is they tell you what it means. But my psychiatrist said I have two personalities.

Anyway within a couple of days of my brother's death I was using Heroin. There was an addict in the family, I had watched him use it, knew where he kept it and just got on with it. All of my feelings disappeared. As soon as they came back I took some more. I was twelve years old.

I hate this person who never bothered to hide his habit from me. He was supposed to look after me and my mum! If he had been a real man I would not have been in jail and I would not have been a smack head.

Angry ! Too fucking right I am.

Sorry about that, not that it matters. I am slowly learning from talking to Billy the tree that because of the drugs or as I said to him my brother's death, that I stopped being a child, never became an adolescent and never learnt how to grow up.

I am a twelve year old girl in man's clothes who knows how to get what she wants by frightening people. I wonder why my mum stands by me, perhaps she blames herself, perhaps she shares the blame, perhaps she feels the need to protect me as I tried to protect my brother and sisters. One day I might ask her.

So back to me, I listen to the officer. She is trying so hard to get people, that is, other officers to give me a chance. Why should they be convinced by what she is saying? Every time I have been given a chance its gone tits up. It is now down to me. I have so often dished it out now perhaps I need to take the shit that is coming my way.

There is so much more left to say, there are other issues of unresolved grief, there are many new skills to learn, there are many obstacles to overcome. I am working on control, my self-control, my image, other people's responses to me, anger management, you name it I am trying it. Why? I have had enough, there is someone I love who I need to look after, I can not do it the way I am, hopefully if I can 'grow up' I can get it right.

It has taken thirty-two years for me to become who I am. I am at a time when I do not know who I am. The only thing I am sure of is that I am changing. At first I did not want to. I have always resisted change, I used to think that I was happy, in control, untouchable. Now I do not seem to have a choice. It is hard to admit but I need these people who I have mentioned to support me, even protect me.

Think and believe what you want. I do not blame you. As for me I am trying to change, I am trying to be in control by controlling myself and I am trying to take responsibility for my own actions and accept that I need to use my brain not my reputation or fists to make a future for myself and those I care for.

The Last Battle

XH

She is reading one of the books on the desk, isolated from the world. The window next to her means nothing at all, she hardly notices it. It's not that it is small and invisible. It is bright and clean and transparent. There are kids running out there and their happy joy is carried on the winds. But she won't lift her eye and even glance at the window.

She is rushing to finish her homework but it seems that it would never be finished. It has been ten years of study, her vital exam coming next month. On this depends whether she will go to university or stay in this town; whether she will have a bright future or have to pick up a non-skilled job. All this depends on this next battle.

By this window, under this pressure she has been through three unforgettable preparations for exams that helped her through primary and secondary School. Almost every night she has sat in this place regardless of what is going on outside. Sometimes the window is slightly open, sometimes it is open wide. Only occasionally is it shut when it is pouring with heavy rain. She needs the fresh air to keep her mind clear.

She has returned to deep thinking after her mind became uncontrollable, flying away. But she has stirred herself and comes back to deep thinking. She might want to look out of the window in a languishing mood more often. But she had to avoid looking out of the window, stop her mind moving through it right now. She needs to work hard now, not later. If she wants to relax and have a nice life in the future she has to work hard in the present. And that moment has lasted ten years already.

She couldn't lose these last stressful moments in this battle.

Definitely not.

new bridge

Lesley Dixon

Funded by the national prisoners' charity, New Bridge, the Learning Shop at Low Newton hosts a unique learning opportunity, providing an element of personal choice while acknowledging the challenges surrounding the acquisition of new knowledge and skills within a system such as that at Low Newton. On the national scene New Bridge's principle aim is to provide links between the learner and community by maintaining family contact and creating voluntary opportunities for learners to increase their self esteem by the opportunity to acquire new skills which will assist in their successful re-integration into society.

The Learning Shop's unique environment provides an element of personal choice and an opportunity to work on an individual basis. The Learners come from diverse environmental, social and increasingly, geographical backgrounds; they have a broad range of abilities. Staffed by three workers, The Learning Shop creates learning opportunities for some of the most isolated and vulnerable women within Low Newton. Staff from Durham County Library Services encourage users with a unique blend of enthusiasm and humour and are an essential component within the team.

In the last year, the Writer In Residence, Wendy Robertson, has based herself in the Learning Shop, working with individuals and small workshop groups to encourage original writing. The writers come from all parts of Low Newton. Many of them have sustained their interest in this work and have developed their writing and self expression. It is good to note an increase in communication, collaboration and self esteem on the part of those who continue to participate.

One special voluntary opportunity organised by the Writer In Residence, 'The Litfest Inside' (an event designed to reflect the Durham Literature Festival in the city outside) was mounted by the Learning Shop to encourage individuals to experience reading and writing at its most exciting level. Within two weeks seven published writers came in to give talks and present workshops enabling Learners, staff and volunteers to meet with and share the experiences of this group of published authors as they explored the motivating factors and experiences of a writer.

The process was facilitated and supported by our resident published writers Wendy Robertson and Avril Joy. Clearly the writing and the exchange of views and ideas continue to have a lasting impact on all participants.

Now this volume, THE SELF REVEALED, showcases the range of original writing achieved at Low Newton writers both in the Learning Shop and from the wider Low Newton community. Its contents reflect the New Bridge principles of developing individual skills, raising self esteem and offering supportive respect for individual experiences.

Lesley Dixon
Manager, Learning Shop